A FAITH-FILLED JOURNEY
TO BECOMING WHO **GOD**
CALLED YOU TO BE

estified

S EPS

ESTHER JOY

Paperback ISBN: 979-8-89741-008-8
Hardcover ISBN: 979-8-89741-019-4
eBook ISBN: 979-8-89741-009-5

For permission requests, please contact:

The 1 and Only
4500 Forbes Boulevard, STE 200
Lanham, MD 20706
www.the1andonlypublishing.com

Contents

Introduction

IN THE DARK HOURS well before the dawn, I sat—laptop warm, heart brimming with purpose—to craft the introduction for this book. My earnest desire was for God's gracious guidance. I prayed, "Lord, what should I do next? Please provide me with creative ideas for Your glory."

For an entire year, I've been paralyzed by fear, haunted by the shadows of my past. A devastating business failure left scars that run deep to this day. Yet, even in my vulnerability, I've realized that God speaks to His children through the most unexpected channels. Dreams, sermons, scriptures, conversation, even social media clips. God's communication knows no bounds; we must be attuned to recognize His voice.

After lifting my prayer, I felt Him speak again and a profound shift occurred. A weight had been lifted. That night I drifted into an intensely vivid dream where a young woman revealed her journey of creating a book aimed at helping others reflect on their walk with Christ and record personal testimonies that uplift faith. Her words ignited a spark, and I woke with a jolt of clarity—I was meant to help others recount their journeys with Christ. Tears of joy streamed down my face as I was overwhelmed by the magnitude of this revelation. Overwhelmed by gratitude, I felt a powerful sense of divine obedience wash over me.

With renewed purpose, I grabbed my laptop and began to write this introduction, eager to share the inspiring message entrusted to me. Often on our walk, the weight of this life presses hard upon us. Like the children of Israel during their time of wandering, our hunger and thirst in the wilderness seasons of life can cause us to forget how the Lord has moved mightily for us, creating an environment of discontentment and discouragement. We may even consider giving up on our journey to the Promised Land.

My father, a minister, expressed his frustration to me once about not feeling God's favor. He shared his current struggles, but as I probed into his past, he began to recount powerful moments when God's favor had been evident in his life—stories I had never heard before. In recounting his testimony to me, it not only empowered my faith but also reignited his.

We often see famous preachers and influencers sharing their testimonies on grand platforms, but what about the usher who has served the Lord for over twenty years? What about the new believer who has experienced a profound move of God in their life? What about the mother who intercedes for strangers in the early morning hours? We each have a story; God is moving in all our lives. The Bible recounts the incredible life stories of Joseph, David, and Paul—remarkable examples of individuals sharing their journeys with the Lord. This is an opportunity to present the 21st-century version of those walks, celebrating the unique ways God works in each of our lives.

In each day of this devotional journal, you will find a scripture, a piece of my own testimony, words of encouragement, questions to prompt your own reflections and space for you to write them down for posterity and future encouragement. You may not see yourself as a writer, but don't let that discourage you. Trade in the pen to video or audio record your experiences with the Lord or find a quiet space in your room to meditate on the moments that have shaped your life since you gave your heart to the Lord. Let your own testimony inspire and encourage you to keep running the race!

Remember, this journal is designed for believers at any stage. You may have newly surrendered your life to the Lord and be wondering, "What do I do now?" Perhaps you dedicated your life to Christ years ago, and the fire you once felt has dimmed. Or you might be a mature believer looking to explore something new on your spiritual journey or seeking a way to share more of your story with your friends and loved ones. Consider this a 30-Day Challenge—Your Walk with Christ. Each day presents an opportunity for reflection, growth, and connection. Together, we will navigate the journey of faith, rekindle the flames of passion, and embrace experiences that have deepened our relationship with God, while seeking His face today.

I pray that during these next thirty days, you fall deeper and deeper in love with the Lord, reminding yourself of how good God has been in your life. You are encouraged to know that YOU ARE NOT ALONE with every word you read. There are people all over the world going through similar experiences, and God got them through it.

Father God, help me as I write this book. Take over this process so that I can help Your people. Holy Spirit, I surrender this to you. In the name of Jesus, Amen!

Origin Story

I tell you that in the same way, there will be
more rejoicing in heaven over one sinner
who repents than over ninety-nine righteous
persons who do not need to repent.

LUKE 15:7 (NIV)

WE EACH HAVE A UNIQUE STORY of how we came to the Lord. While every
one of God's children is known, elected, and called by Him, no two
testimonies are the same. Some were born right into a family of believers and grew up with a lifetime knowledge of Jesus. Others find Him
in college or well into adulthood. Many have a combination of the two
stories, raised in church but falling away, only for the Shepherd to gently lead them back years later.

Whether you were raised in Sunday school or read the Bible for the
first time after years of wondering if there was more to life, every story

matters. Today, I'll share my salvation experience, then give you space to share yours.

I was born into the Christian lifestyle, but that doesn't mean I've always served God. The daughter of an immigrant minister, we didn't have much, and I felt the burden of caring for my family from a young age. My parents did what they could, but I despised the ridicule we bore unable to keep up with the latest designer trends of my New York City classmates.

By thirteen, I was determined to earn money for myself. I landed my first job at a daycare, earning $100 a week for working 3 hours every day after school. Soon, I was dressing like my friends, and I even made enough to buy designer clothes for my younger brother, shielding him from the mockery I'd endured.

Through it all, my parents did their best, providing for us in every way they could, but we lived paycheck to paycheck—getting by but never genuinely flourishing. As I grew older, I understood the toll this took and resolved to break the cycle of struggle. I would pave my own path to financial freedom for my family.

First, I tried launching several businesses while advancing in my corporate career; some earned a little, but nothing ever took off. Then, I was presented with what I believed to be a life-changing opportunity: a legal indoor cannabis farm in Oklahoma. It felt like my big break. With my background in finance, I was thrilled at the potential for substantial earnings. It was a risk, but I understood that and took a leap of faith, securing a second mortgage on my home and depleting my savings to invest in this venture. I dove in headfirst, fully committed.

By the end of the next year, it became painfully apparent that my business was failing. I lost everything. Not only were my finances in turmoil, but every aspect of my life, from relationships to my physical well-being, had been careening toward destruction long before I even embarked on that final business venture. I had tried numerous things to fill the void within me—relationships, drugs, parties, and throwing myself into my career. Yet, nothing could bring me true happiness or peace.

After nights filled with drinking and dancing, I would wake up the next day feeling a profound sadness, or even depression. Though my outward appearance radiated pleasure, I felt utterly broken and empty. In desperation, I turned to the one place I had strayed from for so long—church. My brother, who was actively serving at a local church, encouraged me to attend. Having no other alternative, I decided to take him up on his offer. It had been almost seventeen years since I had last set foot in a church. I was very uncomfortable at even the idea.

Nevertheless, desperation spurred me on, and I began attending services. While physically present in the pews, I was not genuinely engaged until one cold Sunday in January— a day that changed everything for me. The minister concluded his sermon and handed the microphone to his wife. It was the first time I had seen her take the stage. As she began to worship the Lord with her sweet voice, a powerful presence filled the sanctuary.

With my eyes closed, I joined in, letting the music wash over me. Each time she spoke, I felt an overwhelming sense of pure love unlike anything I had ever experienced. Words cannot fully convey the magnitude of what the Holy Spirit was working within me. For the first time since I returned to church, an altar call was presented. She invited anyone who wished to surrender their life to the Lord to come forward. At that moment, I felt an irresistible urge to move. I was no longer in control; the Holy Spirit directed my feet as I approached the altar. Tears streamed down my face, and I could sense the Lord wrapping His arms around me.

At that moment I knew what I had been looking for the last seventeen years—LOVE. Not the kind of love you get from your parents or friends but a love that is unmovable and unshakeable. A love that you don't have to earn. A love you can never lose. The kind of love that breaks strongholds and ends wars. A love that is indescribable, but if I had to try, it would be in the words of Paul.

Love is patient, love is kind, it does not envy it does not boast, it is not proud. It does not dishonor others, it is not self-seeking, it is not easily angered, it keeps no record of wrongs. Love does not delight in evil but rejoices with the truth. It always protects, always trusts, always hopes, always perseveres. Love never fails! (1 Cor. 13:8)

At that altar, I heard the Holy Spirit whisper three profound words, "I got you." In that instant, I found myself crying uncontrollably. The weight of family responsibilities and burdens melted away, and I knew, without a doubt, that I was His.

Each of us has a unique testimony detailing what brought us to the Lord. Reflecting on that pivotal experience is incredibly powerful. Even as I write this passage, I sincerely appreciate the transformative time that reshaped my beliefs and priorities.

Each story we carry holds the power to inspire and uplift those around us, serving as a reminder of God's relentless love and grace.

Reflect on the moment that brought you to the Lord. What transpired during that time? Perhaps it was a life-altering event—a moment of crisis, loss, or profound realization that left you searching for something greater. Maybe it was a gradual awakening, where subtle nudges from the Holy Spirit began to stir your heart. Consider the circumstances surrounding your conversion.

Was there a specific sermon, testimony, or encounter that resonated deeply with you? Did a friend or family member's unwavering faith ignite a spark of curiosity?

What feelings arose as you began to explore your faith? Did elements of fear, hope, or longing compel you toward God?

As you reflect on that significant moment, consider how it has influenced your journey. How has your testimony grown and evolved?

_____

_____

_____

_____

_____

_____

_____

Begin

I want to know Christ—yes, to know the power of his resurrection and participation in his sufferings, becoming like him in his death.

— PHILIPPIANS 3:10 [NIV]

AFTER COMING TO CHRIST, we are new creatures. Yet, the full knowledge of our Savior is not something the Lord gives us all at once. Our walk with Jesus is relational and progressive. All relationships are built from the ground up. Those with a strong foundation are based first on deep-level discovery. To build a lasting connection, we spend time getting to know the new person in our lives. What are their likes and dislikes? What are their core values? We spend hours in conversation. Building our bond with the Savior is no different, except its benefits are eternal.

The day after recommitting my life to Christ, I penned this heartfelt prayer in my journal: "Dear Lord, my Father, my friend, Your goodness is overwhelming. Your Spirit resides within me, and I eagerly await Your voice. As I drift into sleep, Your words surround my thoughts. Please help me understand You better; sometimes, Your words confuse me. All I desire is a deeper connection with You."

In the following weeks, I filled my journal with more entries, echoing my longing for a deeper connection. The experience mirrored that which I had experienced in romantic relationships. For me, falling in love has always been an all-consuming undertaking. I ask a million questions trying to get to know the person, even studying their facial expressions to discern their innermost thoughts. I desire to be as close as possible. In the past, my fascination often bordered on obsession.

After surrendering my life to the Lord, my love for Him felt equally intense and consuming. I canceled all my streaming subscriptions except for YouTube, immersing myself in teaching after teaching from pastors and speakers who I hoped would teach me about my Savior. I was eager to absorb every ounce of knowledge about Him that I could. Despite my efforts, I still felt lost and confused when I opened my Bible to read. The sheer size of His Word and the vastness of what there was to learn felt overwhelming. I jumped around from Genesis to Matthew, then to Proverbs, and back to Genesis again, wandering through the text without absorbing what I needed to feed my soul. It was a whirlwind of scripture, but I craved a clearer path for my spiritual journey.

Blessed with two parents in the ministry, I was able to share my frustrations with my father. He gently recommended I start with the book of John. The recounting of the profound events surrounding Jesus' life and ministry by one of His own disciples began unraveling what Jesus did for me. The message He brought provides a solid foundation to illuminate the other books of the Bible, including the Old Testament, all of which point us to Him. With my father's guidance, I felt a sense of direction and purpose in my pursuit of knowledge.

We are in an extraordinary time of significant revelations emerging from all corners of the earth and easily accessible. While relying solely on others' perspectives is tempting, the Lord also desires to nurture our relationship with Him directly. A true connection with Him teaches us to recognize His voice, opening the path to hear revelations uniquely suited to our lives, shining light on the distinct path He has created for each of his children.

When a testimony is shared, who would you rather hear it from—someone merely recounting a story they've heard or the person who walked through the experience? I would prefer to hear it straight from the source. This preference underscores the importance of direct communication and engagement with God, which leads to great insights and a richer understanding of our faith. He desires to speak to His children and uses multiple paths to do so. While He has called some to ministry to shed light for many, He also desires to speak directly to the hearts of those who serve Him in individual revelation.

God told His people in Jeremiah 33:3, "Call to me and I will answer you and tell you great and unsearchable things you do not know."

Jesus tells us His sheep hear His voice and know it. When we seek Him, we will find Him. While He is the God of all the universe and our feeble human understanding will never fully grasp the magnitude of His greatness, walking daily with Him will teach us to know Him and the power of His resurrection. Knock and the door will be opened. Ask and He will answer.

After coming to Christ, how did He begin to reveal more of who He is to you? Perhaps it started with a significant experience—like a powerful sermon, a moment of worship, or a life-changing event that sparked your curiosity about Him.

What steps did you take in those early days to deepen your relationship with God? Many new believers begin with the Gospels, eager to learn about the life and teachings of Jesus. Did you start with the book of John, captivated by its deep expressions of love and grace? Or did you turn to the Psalms, finding solace in the heartfelt cries and praises that echoed your emotions?

Which scriptures stood out to you in those formative moments? Was there a particular verse that seemed to leap off the page, speaking directly to your heart and guiding you in your newfound faith? How did you respond—by joining a Bible study group, talking with other believers, or spending quiet time in prayer and reflection?

These moments often become pivotal in deepening our understanding and allowing God to reveal more of Himself. Take time to record the passages and practices that helped shape your faith—and thank God for how far He's brought you.

Forgive

**Bear with each other and forgive one another if any
of you has a grievance against someone.
Forgive as the Lord forgave you.**

COLOSSIANS 3:13 [NIV]

FROM THE FIRST DAYS OF HIS MINISTRY, Jesus began bringing people together. Fishermen and tax collectors. A zealot and a woman of ill repute. All were called out from their former lives and into Jesus' inner circle for their souls to be transformed. It couldn't have been easy. Having come from such vastly different backgrounds, tensions were sure to rise amongst a group living so closely together, traveling town to town and through the countryside following Jesus. Who would sit at His right and left hand in glory would've been merely one of a great many points of contention.

Following His resurrection, diversity in the church only increased as Gentiles were brought into the saving knowledge of Christ. Through it all, the resounding message in the scriptures is to love one another. Forsake not the assembling of yourselves together. Serve and encourage your brother and sister. Bear one another's burdens. Forgive. This is the church. Yet so many find themselves experiencing their worst hurt in the very place they come to find healing—within the community of God's own people.

I spent my childhood deeply involved in the church. With my father as the head pastor of a Pentecostal congregation, I sometimes found myself in church multiple days a week. I even had the opportunity to teach Sunday school. Living in the vibrant landscape of New York City, my parents did their best to keep me on a short leash. At times, it felt like I was living in a bubble. While I had friends in school, my closest companions were primarily other kids from the church. Those experiences forged a unique bond and shaped my worldview.

College brought me a newfound sense of freedom. Though I had experimented with drinking and smoking in high school, it was during my first year at college that I truly got drunk for the first time. I embraced the stereotype of "rebellious pastor's kid." However, in my sophomore year, life took an unexpected turn. At nineteen, I found myself pregnant. This pivotal moment forced me to face the consequences of my choices and changed the course of my future.

I clearly remember the moment a Planned Parenthood clinician said, "Congratulations! You're pregnant." Tears streamed down my face as I lost control there in the office. In desperate need of consolation, I went to the campus sanctuary to pray. To my surprise, a friend was already there. God had sent her to comfort me in my distress and she guided me to call the people I needed in that moment the most—my parents.

Breaking the news to them was heart-wrenching. They were utterly devastated. My father--angry and worried--told me to come home. Without thinking twice, I booked the first Greyhound back to NYC, my heart heavy with uncertainty about what lay ahead. My family decided it was best for me to stay home permanently until my son was born, and, out of obedience, I agreed.

Eventually, word of my pregnancy spread throughout the church. While many greeted me with smiles and some friends offered support, their words often carried an undercurrent of quiet judgment. Others no longer wanted me around their children—people who had once helped raise me. I knew my father loved me, but during that time, he could barely look me in the eye. The weight of it all left me feeling completely alone, trapped in a situation that seemed to sever the bond I once shared with my community.

Following the birth of my son, my family chose to relocate to a different state to start a new church. The pain and loneliness I experienced during that period brought me to a harsh realization: God and the church were not for me. To shield myself from further pain, I distanced myself from both for seventeen years. I abandoned this crucial chapter of my life, seeking comfort in a space free from the echoes of my past struggles.

You've likely heard the phrase, "The church is a hospital." While one might envision the church as filled with caring individuals with the best intentions, this isn't always the reality. It's a place for broken, hurting people who sometimes hurt people. Jesus told the Pharisees "It is not the healthy who need a doctor but the sick. But go and learn what this means: 'I desire mercy not sacrifice.' For I have not come to call the righteous, but sinners." (Matt. 9:12-13)

Every community, including the church, is full of people facing their own struggles, insecurities, and flaws. It's not our duty to change these individuals—that's for the Lord to address. Our role is to offer mercy, love, and forgiveness.

Have you ever been hurt by someone within your church community? Perhaps it was a sharp criticism, a misunderstanding that grew beyond your control, or a betrayal of trust that left you wounded. These experiences can be deeply painful, stirring feelings of frustration, disappointment, or even disillusionment—especially when they come from a community meant to nurture and uplift.

How did you respond at that moment? Did you seek resolution with the person involved, or did you quietly carry the hurt, unsure how to process it?? Pride, fear, or uncertainty may keep us from reaching out or speaking honestly in our pain.

As you look back, how did healing begin? Once you processed your feelings, were you able to move toward forgiveness? Remember, forgiveness is often a journey—not a one-time decision. Extending grace toward others—and to ourselves—is a vital part of nurturing our spiritual health.

Take a moment to reflect. Are there wounds you're still carrying? Invite God into the hurt, and write out a prayer asking for healing, grace, and the strength to let go of any lingering bitterness. You are not alone—He is close to the brokenhearted.

Identity

**But you are a chosen people, a royal priesthood,
a holy nation, God's special possession that you
may declare the praises of him who called you
out of darkness into his wonderful light.**

ᦉ 1 PETER 2:9 (NIV)

THE MESSAGE TODAY is not only loud, its permeating. Be anything you want to be. There are no limits. No one can tell you who to be. Yet, instead of empowering society, these messages have created wandering generations that have no roots and great confusion over their identity. Instead of one way to God, the world screams there is no right way—each should choose for themselves. "Wide is that gate ... that leads to destruction." (Matthew 7:13)

The question of identity is one I frequently grappled with throughout my early life. Before committing my life to the Lord, I struggled deeply to know who I truly was and find my purpose. I was a sponge, soaking up the character of those around me. I subconsciously adopted their identities. I began to mimic their speech, make similar decisions, and ultimately, think like them. Occasionally, the people I emulated were admirable, leading me to engage in positive behaviors. However, I also associated with individuals whose lifestyles only led to ruin. Although I attempted to uphold a personal standard, I often found myself teetering between right and wrong, unknowingly inviting chaos into my life.

After dedicating my life to the Lord, the initial excitement quickly shifted to an important question: Who am I? Surrendering to Christ sparks a fervor and enthusiasm that fills you with a desire to know Him deeply, directing your focus entirely on Him. You yearn for more of Jesus, immersing yourself in His presence. Zeal can be tenuous though and, for many, the passion ebbs and flows, often veering toward the waning. I realized that, like a sponge, if I had devoted more time to reading His Word and reveling in His presence as I do now, I would have naturally started resembling my friend, Jesus Christ. Instead, I let the enemy invade my thoughts, whispering that I am insignificant and unworthy of love or acceptance.

My ultimate resolution was to go through the Bible and discover who I truly was in Christ. I began meditating on specific scriptures every day—proclaiming truth over my life until it took root in my heart.

I am chosen –
"You did not choose me, but I chose you and appointed you..."
(John 15:16)

I am free –
"So if the Son sets you free, you will be free indeed." (John 8:36)

I am redeemed –
"In Him we have redemption through His blood,
the forgiveness of sins..."
(Ephesians 1:7)

I am His –
"Fear not, for I have redeemed you;
I have called you by name, you are mine."
(Isaiah 43:1)

These declarations were written on notes I placed on my mirror, so I would see and speak them every time I looked at myself. Over time, those words became more than just affirmations—they became part of who I am.

Understanding your identity in the Lord is a vital foundation for standing firm in your faith. Recognizing how God sees you shapes the way you view yourself and influences how you navigate life's challenges. When you root your sense of self in Him as one who is loved, chosen, and redeemed, you no longer chase after the things that cannot satisfy—performance, comparison, and approval from others. In Christ, we find true freedom. We are made in His image and, when we find ourselves returning to our true identity in Him, we are no longer bound by the confusion an unstable sense of self brings. Embracing your identity as a new creature in Christ brings clarity, peace, and purpose to your soul. Knowing who you are in Him forms your life in a way that is empowering and freeing.

Reflect on a specific moment when your eyes were truly opened, and you began to grasp who you are in Christ. Maybe it was through a verse that seemed written just for you, a conversation with a trusted mentor, or a powerful encounter during prayer. What shifted in your heart and mind as you realized your identity is rooted not in the world, but in Him?

How did that revelation transform the way you see yourself? What emotions surfaced—freedom, peace, joy, or even discomfort as old beliefs fell away? Consider how this newfound understanding affected your choices, your relationships, and your sense of purpose.

Has knowing your identity in Christ ever given you the courage to stand up for your beliefs? Has it brought healing in areas of past insecurity or shame? Reflect on the fruit this identity has borne in your life, and how it continues to shape the way you live. In every season, your identity in Christ remains constant—a source of strength, direction, and belonging. Let this truth anchor your heart as you walk with Him.

_____

_____

_____

_____

_____

_____

Transformation

**You were taught, about your former way of life,
to put off your old self, which is being corrupted by
its deceitful desires; to be made new in the attitude
of your minds; and to put on the new self, created
to be like God in true righteousness and holiness.**

      EPHESIANS 4:22-24 [NIV]

THOSE FIRST DAYS OR WEEKS of committing a new life to Christ are a glorious, mountaintop experience. But life isn't lived in the mountaintops. There are valleys to walk through and sooner rather than later, every Christian finds old habits and ways creeping back in—sometimes slowly, other times in full force. Even Paul, an apostle of Christ, commiserated saying he knows what he should do at times yet doesn't, and other times does what he shouldn't do. How relatable!

Shortly after I recommitted my life to Christ, I wrote in my journal:

"Dear Lord, I have sinned. I spent the night with HIM. I want to promise I'll never do it again, but I would be lying, and you already know my heart. So, I repent to you and ask for the strength to stop. Help me quit smoking, reduce my drinking, and distance myself from friends of negative influence at this time. I struggle with all of that. I genuinely want to draw closer to you, but it's challenging knowing my sins. Father, please help me become more robust. Please help me choose You every day. Lord, You are so faithful and merciful. I want to improve for You and make You happy. Lord! Please help me! Your loving daughter, Amen."

Many mistakenly believe that dedicating their life to the Lord will cause all sinful behaviors to disappear. They also think that when they sin, the Lord becomes displeased and abandons them. Our struggle does not make our salvation any less real or prove our love for Christ false. It makes us humans in constant need of grace and proves our desperate need for a Savior.

The love of a good parent—whether received or given—offers us a small but powerful glimpse of our Heavenly Father's love. A parent carefully instructs and nurtures their child, teaching them what is right and beneficial, hoping they will choose to obey. Yet, so often, children go against that guidance and do exactly what they were warned not to. Though parents may correct or discipline, their love remains steadfast and unwavering.

Even if that child keeps repeating the same errors, the parents may experience frustration or disappointment, but the love of a good mother or father never stops. Time and time again the scripture shows us that God is not just our Heavenly Father, but He is a good Father, providing for His children, instructing them and yes, when necessary, correcting them. Matthew records Jesus as saying that if human fathers can take care of their children, how much more can the Heavenly Father take good care of us? (Matt. 7:11)

No matter how we respond, it's crucial to remember that human emotions or boundaries do not apply to God. As a Spirit, He remains eternally aware of our decisions even before we make them. His love is unconditional and exceeds the misunderstandings that often stem from human experiences. Rather than abandoning us during our failures, God's love stays unwavering, giving us grace and the chance for redemption. Recognizing this can enhance our connection with the divine, urging us to return to Him, regardless of how frequently we falter.

The belief that God is angry when His children stumble fosters a sense of shame and unworthiness that create a significant divide between God and His chosen people. When I offered that prayer just nine days after surrendering my life to the Lord, I held the belief that continuing to sin would make me unwanted by Him and that I was worthless in His sight. Biblically, sin is sin in God's eyes. Whether someone commits murder or simply spreads gossip, all sin carries the same weight and, because of God's righteousness, requires atonement. This understanding reveals that we are all vulnerable to sin, sometimes knowingly and other times unknowingly, reinforcing our desperate need for a Savior.

It says in Romans 5:20, "Where sin increased, grace increased all the more." In the next chapter, Paul is quick to clarify we are not to exploit God's grace by going on sinning so that grace may increase. Our transformation isn't a one-time experience. The renewing of our minds comes through an ongoing walk with Him. We are all a work in progress. When we sin and feel the Holy Spirit's conviction, we shouldn't ignore it; we should take it to God. Seek His forgiveness and the strength to resist sin in the future grows. Expressing our gratitude to the Lord for revealing these issues to us is vital. As David asked, He can cleanse us even from our secret faults. He wants us to be open and honest to experience His love, grace, and mercy more profoundly. Realizing that we are always a work in progress allows us to accept God's transformative power in our lives.

As babes in Christ, we may think sin creates a gap between us and God. Guilt and shame can lead us to feel distant from His love. As we grow in faith, we learn that God's mercy and grace cover us, reassuring us of His desire for a relationship despite our shortcomings. Recalling along the journey where He's brought us from and where we could have been reminds us of His great love with which He loves us.

Think back to a time when sin created a sense of distance between you and the Lord. What did that experience feel like? Maybe the aftermath of your actions left you in despair, struggling to connect with Him through prayer or worship. Did you withdraw, feeling unworthy of His love or favor? These emotions are common—especially early in our walk with Christ—when we're still learning how to carry the weight of our humanity in light of His grace.

How did you handle that moment? Did you turn to God and seek forgiveness, or did shame hold you back? It's essential to recognize how easily guilt can become a barrier and how the enemy often uses it to keep us from the very One who offers the healing and restoration we desperately need.

Then reflect on when you realized the perceived distance wasn't from God pulling away. What opened your eyes to that truth? Was it a sermon, a conversation with a trusted friend? Maybe a profound realization during your quiet time with the Lord. Did you begin to understand that God's love is not contingent on our perfection but instead rooted in His unchanging nature?

After embracing that truth, how did your relationship change? Did you return to the Lord with a renewed passion for prayer, worship, and Scripture? How did you incorporate the practices of confession and repentance into your spiritual routine?

Take time now to write honestly about your experience—and consider offering a prayer of gratitude to the God who welcomes us back again and again with open arms.

_____

_____

DAY 6:

Friendship

**Do not be yoked together with unbelievers. For what
do righteousness and wickedness have in common?
Or what fellowship can light have with darkness?**

∽ 2 CORINTHIANS 6:14 (NIV)

AS WE BECOME NEW CREATURES IN CHRIST, we are changed from the old into the new. There may be parts of the past—friends and even family—who do not resonate with the transformation. Friends from our former life often fail to understand the change taking place within us and turn away. Or worse, as fledgling believers we try to hide our newfound faith and walk the thin line between serving God and maintaining parts of our old lives. We assume we can find some sort of happy balance between the two.

After my rededication, I had a dream that profoundly impacted me. In the dream, I left my peaceful home for an exciting night out with friends. As luck would have it, it grew too late to head back, and we ended up at the house of one of the women. As I entered her home, filled with many rooms and roommates, an overwhelming sense of discomfort flooded me—an eerie feeling I couldn't shake. While my friends settled in and fell asleep, I remained wide awake, wrestling with these troubling emotions. I sat in the kitchen and attempted to unravel the root of my unease.

Before long, one of her roommates came home. When I saw her, I felt the urge to tell her I couldn't sleep because I felt a strong, evil presence in the house. To my surprise, she admitted that she was also having trouble sleeping and pointed out that the house was filled with unbelievers.

This dream occurred shortly after I chose to go out with my friends rather than attending church. In truth, I had been balancing that thin line between my old life and the new, trying to keep a foothold in both. I felt torn between maintaining closeness with friends and remained involved in worldly activities while simultaneously trying to focus on Jesus. Deep down, I genuinely believed I would be able to hold onto both, with my faith equipping me to fend off the negative influences while enjoying the benefits of the relationships I'd been accustomed to.

Nevertheless, the unease I felt in my dream deeply reflected my inner conflict. Focusing on socializing instead of spiritual nourishment exposed me to that struggle, which the dream vividly manifested. It underscored that balancing worldly pursuits with a dedication to Christ can result in spiritual distress. God speaks in the quiet spaces, and this would be the first time of many He would come to me in the night to reveal an area in my life with which I was struggling.

Setting clear boundaries and seeking joyous fellowship as we grow in our faith is a crucial step for every child of God. Solomon tells us that to become wise we must walk with the wise, and a friend of fools suffers harm. (Prov. 13:20) To grow in Christ, our closest relationships should be with others who share that desire. Choosing deliberately to align with our beliefs is crucial for maintaining a solid connection with God in the beginning of your walk. This dream inspired me to reflect on my priorities and evaluate how my decisions impacted my spiritual path. It urged me to fully embrace life in Christ while acknowledging that some relationships might hinder my growth in this new faith journey. That first year, I experienced a significant shift in my friendships.

Some relationships gradually diminished, while I consciously chose to separate from others. The apostle Paul said it plainly in 1 Corinthians 15:33, "Bad company ruins morals." Although this was difficult, it became essential to my spiritual journey. I'm not suggesting that we end friendships with people with different beliefs; instead, I emphasize the need for clear boundaries in those connections. The guardrail at the side of a winding mountain pass isn't to keep travelers from enjoying the drive but to protect them from veering over the edge. Proper boundaries protect and nurture healthy relationships. As we work to strengthen our faith and align with our principles, we must set guidelines that guard and improve our spiritual health.

Have you ever struggled with maintaining old friendships while stepping into a new direction with God? What emotions surfaced during that season of change? Perhaps you felt torn—caught between the warmth of shared memories and the pull to stay aligned with your growing faith.

Think about the specific relationships that tested your resolve. Was there someone you deeply cared for but recognized their influence no longer nurturing your spiritual growth? How did you navigate that tension? Did you sense the Holy Spirit gently nudging you to redefine or even distance yourself from that connection?

Letting go is never easy, especially when those friendships have historically brought a sense of comfort. But sometimes, staying close to God requires courageous obedience. Old friends evoke comfort and familiarity, even when they no longer glorify the Lord. Are there relationships in your life today that need protective boundaries to preserve your walk with the Lord?

Use this time to reflect honestly. Write about your experience, your emotions, and how God led you through—or is still leading you through—those decisions. Ask Him for wisdom, strength, and peace as you seek relationships that honor both Him and the Christ-follower He's shaping you to become.

Authority

**I have given you authority to trample on snakes
and scorpions and to overcome all the power
of the enemy; nothing will harm you.**

LUKE 10:19 (NIV)

LUKE RECORDS IN CHAPTER 9 OF HIS GOSPEL that Jesus called his twelve disciples together and gave them power and authority to drive out demons and cure diseases. Yet a few verses later, a man brings his possessed son to Christ, saying the disciples had tried to drive the evil spirits out of him but failed. Matthew takes the story further by revealing the disciples came to Jesus privately after He had delivered the boy, asking why they were unable to drive it out. Their teacher told them clearly, "Because you have so little faith" (Matt. 17:20a).

I recall a vivid dream that left a profound mark on me. In this dream, I found myself inside a house filled with windows and doors.

Upon entering, I immediately sensed something strange about the owner. There was a disturbing aura around him that hinted at evil, yet I couldn't figure out his true intentions. He mentioned needing to step out for a moment and asked me to wait in his house. I complied, but my discomfort intensified as I realized that all the windows and doors were either unlocked or open, except for the front door, which stood firmly closed.

Suddenly, there was a knock at the door. When I peered through the peephole, I immediately sensed a dark presence. It was a witch. But as soon as she noticed me, she transformed into the appearance of a beautiful woman. Panic surged within me as I hurried from the door to the window, locking each one in a frantic bid for safety. However, as I approached the balcony door, she somehow managed to break in, reverting to her true form as a witch. Terror engulfed me! In a desperate attempt to escape this nightmare, I grabbed my phone to call my mom, but there was no answer. I tried my dad next, but there was still no answer. In a fit of fear, my voice trembling, I cried out, "In the name of Jesus!" Abruptly, I woke up.

Reflecting on this dream, I realized I once lacked confidence in my spiritual authority. I didn't fully understand the significance of my role in the spiritual realm or the strength that comes from my identity in Christ. I was oblivious to the fact that I was seated at the Lord's right hand, part of the body of Christ, possessing dominion over all powers, principalities, and demons. Everything lies beneath us. This dream reshaped my view of spiritual authority, prompting me to explore more of who I am in Christ. Today, I accept the truth that I am truly empowered. I aim to live out that authority, resisting fear while embracing the peace that transcends all understanding (Phil. 4:7).

Our authority comes from being in Christ—His power made manifest in us. While it's not something we can earn or deserve, it is through faith in Him and belief in His ultimate authority that we can speak words that cause evil to flee. Jesus told His disciples that if they had faith even as small as a mustard seed, nothing would be impossible for them (Matt. 17:20b). It doesn't take a lot of faith—the mustard seed is a tiny seed that grows into a mighty tree. But it takes faith in the right person.

To have full faith in Jesus, we must know Him. We learn who He is and how His power is made manifest in us by going through the tests and trials of this life relying on Him. In our struggle, His true character is revealed—so that we may know Him and the power of His might.

Sometimes we think that only pastors or ministers have the authority to confront evil, leaving the rest of us feeling powerless. But scripture reminds us that every believer, through faith in Christ, carries this authority.

Think back to a time you stepped into that spiritual authority in Christ. Was it during a troubling situation or when you prayed for someone struggling with fear? Did you call on the name of Jesus and step out in faith?

What did you experience at that moment? How did God respond? What changes did you observe—either externally or in your own heart? Did it increase your confidence in His presence and authority? Even small acts of faith can lead to profound results.

Take a moment to ask God: Where am I being called to walk in spiritual authority today? Write down what comes to mind, and pray for the boldness to act on it, trusting that He has already equipped you.

Experiences

> **Then Moses said, 'Now show me your glory.'**
> **And the Lord said, 'I will cause all my goodness**
> **to pass in front of you, and I will proclaim my**
> **name, the Lord, in your presence. I will have**
> **mercy on whom I will have mercy, and I will have**
> **compassion on whom I will have compassion.'**
>
> EXODUS 33:18-19 (NIV)

JESUS PROMISED HIS DISCIPLES that although He would have to go away, He would pray, and the Father would send to them an advocate. He told them clearly to stay in the city until they were clothed in power, and they did just that. God's Spirit fell upon the church in the upper room and incredible miracles and wonders followed. That same Spirit is still alive in the church today, speaking to and working through His people.

The church I attend is a lively community brimming with miracles, signs, wonders, and prophetic messages. It's uplifting to see people prayed for, allowing themselves to fall "under the fire of the Holy Ghost." Others from the congregation often receive insightful, transformative, prophetic words.

As I grew in my relationship with the Lord, I yearned for those experiences. I craved the sensation of falling deeply into the Spirit and the comfort of hearing a personal, prophetic word spoken over my life. However, there were moments of discouragement when these gifts seemed out of reach—given to others and not me. I wrestled with feelings of inadequacy, often questioning, "What is wrong with me? Am I not deserving of this experience?" Such thoughts can easily surface when witnessing others encounter the Holy Spirit in impactful ways while we feel sidelined. In truth, the Lord never sidelines His children, but He doesn't have them all playing the same position either. Each one's gift, journey, and experience will be unique. And while I was questioning, He was crafting a special moment just for me.

One evening, I was captivated by a video of a preacher interacting with a woman in the audience. He declared, "I see the Spirit of Kathryn Kuhlman upon you." The statement resonated profoundly with me. Kathryn Kuhlman and her extraordinary teachings had always inspired me; I truly admired the divine power that flowed through her. His words stirred something within me, prompting a sincere and simple prayer: "Lord, grant me the Spirit of Kathryn Kuhlman. Speak through me as you did with Moses and allow me to see angels like the Prophet Isaiah." I repeated this prayer several times, pouring my heart into it, longing for a deeper relationship with God and the transformative influence of the Holy Spirit in my life.

As I kept praying, yearning stirred within me. I knelt, earnestly imploring the Holy Ghost to enter my room and envelop me in His presence. I bared my soul, desiring a divine encounter. Despite my heartfelt pleas, nothing supernatural seemed to occur. The heavens seemed like brass, my prayers pinging the surface unheard and unanswered. A growing tiredness washed over me, making it difficult to sustain the intensity of my prayers. Ultimately, sleep prevailed as the calming sounds of Benny Hinn, recounting his first experience with the Holy Ghost during a Kathryn Kuhlman crusade, played softly in the background.

I awoke suddenly in a trance and found myself at a Benny Hinn conference, surrounded by an atmosphere infused with the Holy Spirit. The presence of God filled me, wrapping me in a warmth and peace that was both overwhelming and exhilarating. An instant later, I was back in my bed slowly coming to an awareness of the state of things around me. My room was uncharacteristically messy, and I sat up, thinking I would take care of it. As I was about to get out of bed, I glanced at my feet and saw stamps from all over the world decorating them. Instinctively I understood that each mark told a story of places I had visited or would visit one day. Alongside these stamps, various names of the Lord were inscribed on my feet—Yeshua, El Shaddai, Jehovah Jireh—each name echoing profound significance and love. Different Bible verses were written alongside them, rich with the promises and truths of Scripture.

As soon as I took in the incredible sight of my decorated feet, I was jolted out of the trance and back in the familiar comfort of my room, still lying in bed. Even as I returned to reality, the sweet presence of the Holy Ghost filled the air with a soothing warmth as His Spirit rested upon me. Overwhelmed by this experience, I felt the urge to kneel. Tears streamed down my cheeks as I wept before the Lord, inundated with gratitude. I was in awe that the Lord had answered my prayer and revealed Himself in such a profound way. Thank you, Lord!

I share my personal experience to emphasize a profound truth: each of us encounters the Lord in a way that is uniquely our own.

God doesn't operate in a one-size-fits-all manner—His approach is deeply personal, intentionally tailored to meet us where we are. While I longed for dramatic moments—a prophetic word or a powerful touch from the Holy Spirit during a church service—God chose to reveal Himself to me in a quieter, more secluded way. And yet, it was just as life changing.

While your experience may not mirror someone else's, it is in no way less valid or important. Just as a good parent handles each child according to their individual personalities and needs, our Heavenly Father knows the best ways and times to reveal Himself to His children. And when He does, you can take comfort and reassurance in the knowledge it is something He did exclusively for you.

Think back to a time when God revealed Himself to you in a tangible way. Did you intentionally seek this experience? Were you praying for clarity, guidance, or simply longing to feel His presence more deeply in your life?

What did those prayers look like? What emotions or desires were present in your heart at the time? Now reflect on the moment when you felt Him respond—how did He reveal Himself? Was it through a quiet peace, a timely word, a shift in perspective, or something more dramatic?

Describe how it unfolded. Often, God's revelations may not be grand spectacles but appear as subtle feelings or insights that leave a lasting impression on us.

How did this moment impact your faith? Did it motivate you to face your circumstances with renewed faith, fueling a desire to explore your relationship with Him more deeply? Perhaps it reshaped your view of prayer, remind you that God listens and responds to the sincere cries of our heart.

Ultimately, these encounters—whether quiet or bold—is a testament to God's intimate involvement in our lives. They remind us that we are not alone on our journey and that His love and guidance are consistently present. Embracing these unique experiences enhances our relationship with the Lord, fostering a more profound sense of belonging and purpose as we walk in faith.

Take some time to write about your experience. How did God meet you, and what did that moment teach you about who He is? How does it continue to shape your relationship with Him today?

DAY 9:

Obedience

**Walk in obedience to all that the Lord your
God has commanded you, so that you may
live and prosper and prolong your days
in the land that you will possess.**

⟋ DEUTERONOMY 5:33 (NIV)

OFTEN, GOD'S INSTRUCTIONS ARE QUITE CLEAR. In the Old Testament, God
told Saul to destroy the Amalekites and "all that belongs to them."
Speaking through His prophet Samuel, God even listed it out for Saul.
There was no question of what Saul was supposed to do. But just a few
verses later we find that Saul spared Agag, the king, and the best of his
sheep and cattle—"everything that was good" (1 Sam. 15:9).

When confronted with his disobedience, Saul's excuse was that he
had spared the best to sacrifice to the Lord. Again, Samuel asks why he
did not obey God's command, and Saul defends himself saying, "But

I did obey the Lord..." (1 Sam. 15:20). He even tries to shift the blame by claiming it was the soldiers who took the sheep, and Saul was afraid to stop them. It's then Samuel makes God's priorities quite clear in verse 22, "Does the Lord delight in burnt offerings and sacrifices as much as in obeying the Lord? To obey is better than sacrifice and to heed is better than the fat of rams."

I believe I could write a whole book on obedience. Reflecting on my past, I realize that with the knowledge I have now, I could have avoided a lot of heartache. At the time, I was a people pleaser who cared deeply about what others thought of me. This often led to situations in which acting on the Lord's promptings meant I had to either upset someone or face negative judgments myself.

I had a friend from church who seemed to know everyone's affairs. Frequently, I found myself unwittingly taking part in her gossip sessions about our fellow church members. Occasionally, I even sought her out, eager for the latest bits of information I knew she had. One day, while listening to an interview with someone who could perceive the spiritual realm, he made a powerful observation, saying, "When we gossip, it's as if we're throwing up, and the enemy is feasting on our vomit."

This vivid imagery resonated with me so deeply that I was filled with conviction. While I always understood gossip was wrong, this new perspective highlighted the seriousness of my actions. In that instant, the Holy Spirit spoke to me clearly, encouraging me to cease my gossiping (1 Cor. 6:10-11).

Resolute, I decided to stop indulging in gossip. Yet, my church friend remained unaware of my choice. She would come to me before services, trying to initiate gossip. I often attempted to redirect the conversation or completely avoid her, but both strategies sometimes failed. In one of those moments, I found myself praying, "Father, I don't want to hurt her feelings. Please help her to stop!" The Holy

Spirit gently replied, "So, you would rather offend Me?" Those words were a wake-up call.

Finally, I found the courage to express my pain over hearing about the private issues of others and conveyed my wish to cease those discussions entirely. Naturally, she was hurt, but I knew it was more important to focus on pleasing the Lord than to concern myself with her feelings.

The Lord tests us to elevate us, seeking to understand our preparedness for the next level of His glory. These tests usually appear as challenges that push us beyond our comfort zones. Regardless of whether a task seems minor or substantial, what He genuinely wants from us is obedience and a readiness to act with faith and trust.

The truth of the story of Saul and the Amalekites is a stark lesson—it doesn't really matter what else we are doing for the Lord if we are in direct disobedience. Except for Agag and the best of the flock, Saul destroyed the Amalekite nation. Partial obedience is disobedience, and because of Saul's actions, God took the kingdom from him that day. "You have rejected the word of the Lord, and the Lord has rejected you as king over Israel!" (1 Sam. 15:26)

Today, we are covered by the blood of Jesus, and He gives more grace. Yet we cannot continue to live in blatant disobedience to God and expect Him to use us for His will. His grace is free, but it was costly—it cost the very life of Jesus. As we seek after Him, we are continually putting to death the rebellious parts of our nature that turn away from God and chase after the desires of sin. In Him we have new life. In Him we have freedom. A life of obedience to God is one filled with joy and purpose, because He always does what's best—if only we will say "yes."

Reflect on a moment when the Lord called you to do something challenging—maybe it was stepping into a new role, sharing your faith with someone, or letting go of something hindering your growth. How did you respond at that time? Did you step forward in obedience, or did uncertainty cause you to hesitate?

If you obeyed, think about the results. Did it lead to personal growth, new opportunities, or a deeper understanding of God's plan? Often, obeying His call opens unexpected doors and reinforces our trust in His guidance.

If you hesitated, take some time to explore the emotions you felt. What fears or doubts held you back? How did you feel in that moment—anxious, conflicted, or unsettled? Recognizing moments of hesitation is as important as celebrating victories. It reveals where God wants to work in us.

Remember, every act of obedience, no matter how small, shapes our journey with the Lord. Even in our hesitation, He is working in us. Trust that He is always using these experiences to help us grow, and that His desire for our spiritual growth is constant. As you reflect, ask God to reveal how He's been faithful in your journey, whether in moments of obedience or hesitation.

DAY 10:

Meditation

But whose delight is in the law of the Lord, and who meditates on his law day and night. That person is like a tree planted by streams of water, which yields its fruit in season and whose leaf does not wither—whatever they do prospers.

℮ PSALM 1:2-3 (NIV)

THERE ARE OVER A DOZEN VERSES in the Bible about meditating on God's word. The majority came from David—"a man after God's own heart." The world today is increasingly loud. Everywhere we turn we are inundated with noise, screens, music, chatter, information, media. The demands placed upon our time schedules and the unhealthy relationship most of society has with their mobile devices, it's no wonder we struggle to hear God's voice above all the things clamoring for our attention.

Yet Joshua tells us in that by keeping God's Word always on our lips and meditating on it "day and night," we will be more able to follow God's ways and find success in Him (Jo. 1:8). Paul told the church in Colossi to let the message of Christ dwell in them richly (Col. 3:16). Meditating and dwelling in God's Word requires more than a few moments of reading over a cup of coffee before the Bible is closed and left on the shelf for the day.

This was an area I found myself struggling in as a Christian who longed to grow closer to my Lord. I tried to shut out the noise—I watched very little TV. The Chosen, a series portraying the life of Christ and His disciples, was a notable exception. Before I started this show, my Bible reading often felt mechanical. I moved from chapter to chapter without fully absorbing the richness and depth of each verse. Although I was gaining knowledge, I sensed that I wasn't receiving the spiritual nourishment I desired.

Frustrated, I turned to the Lord for insight into the true essence of meditating on His Word. I longed to delve deeper than a surface-level interpretation of Scripture and uncover the profound messages that He communicates. In my exasperation, I put my Bible down and decided to watch an episode of The Chosen.

As I watched with an open mind, aware that the Lord communicates in various ways, I was particularly drawn to the portrayal of Matthew, who hadn't grown up studying the Torah. A moment that deeply resonated with me occurred when he turned to Philip, asking where he should begin. Philip's response was striking; he quoted from a Psalm written by King David. Matthew, touched by the words yet uncertain of their significance, voiced his confusion. Philip offered this wise advice: "Reflect on it. Write it down. Contemplate it—meditate on it—until it becomes a part of you."

This moment resonated deeply with me. Philip's guidance captured the core principles of effective meditation. It's not just about reading;

it's an active engagement with the text. Meditation allows God's Word to sink into our minds and hearts, letting the truth of the passages seep into our very being. I came to understand this entails a process of reflection and contemplation, aiming to fully grasp and apply God's Word in our everyday lives. It demands intentional effort—carving out dedicated time to jot down insights, reflect on the verses throughout the day, and invite the Holy Spirit to enhance our understanding.

This thoughtful meditation practice revealed the often-overlooked beauty and depth of Scripture. I started to recognize the importance of letting God's Word resonate within me, reviving my spirit and directing my actions. There is no single "right way" to meditate—but there are some helpful practices that can be employed. Philip's response is similar to the "Lectio Divina" method—traditionally attributed to Origen of Alexandria, an early Christian scholar around 200 AD. A 12-th century monk later outlined the method into a four-step approach: Lectio (read), Meditatio (meditate), Oratio (pray), and Contemplatio (contemplate).

Each Christian can develop their own method based on their learning and thought styles. Choose a passage intentionally based on a current life situation or an area desired for spiritual growth. If you don't know where to start, the Gospels, Psalms or Proverbs are a great launching pad. Read slowly and deliberately. Ask questions like: what does the text reveal about who God is? How did this apply to His people then and how does it apply to my life today? Journaling is a beautiful way to record your meditations—a key piece to this devotional book. Memorize verses from the passage by carrying a card around with you or saving the verse as a background image on your phone where you'll see it frequently. Most importantly, pray. Ask God for understanding, then sit quietly and listen for the Holy Spirit's guidance.

Think back to a moment when you took the time to meditate on the Word. What did the Lord reveal to you during that sacred time? Was there a specific passage or verse that touched your heart and shifted your perspective?

Reflect on the emotions that surfaced as you lingered with the Scripture. Did new insights or connections emerge that changed your perspective? Each verse might have revealed an additional layer of meaning, illuminating aspects of your life you hadn't thought about before. How did those insights challenge, inspire, or encourage you in your walk with God?

Write down specific Scriptures that have spoken to you in seasons of uncertainty, decision-making, or sorrow. Did they offer direction or peace? Meditation often reveals practical truths for our daily lives, illuminating paths toward growth and transformation.

Ultimately, God desires to meet us in His Word. Each moment spent meditating on Scripture is an invitation for a deeper relationship with Him. As His truth takes root in our hearts, we are strengthened to face life's challenges and shine His light more clearly.

Take time now to reflect how God's Word has and is still shaping you today.

Roots

**But he was pierced for our transgressions,
he was crushed for our iniquities; the
punishment that brought us peace was on
him, and by his wounds, we are healed.**

ISAIAH 53:5 (NIIV)

OUR HEARTS ARE LIKE GARDENS, requiring constant care and attention. At times, weeds begin to grow—things that threaten the health of what's good and fruitful. Every gardener knows you can't just cut off the visible part of the weed; it will only grow back. The real issue lies beneath the surface—in the roots. In our Christian Walk, we often recognize the weeds in our hearts and know they must be dealt with. But a quick fix, like running over them with a lawn mower, won't bring true change. Instead, we must allow the Holy Spirit to lead us into the soil of our souls, digging deep to uncover and remove the root causes. It's only when the roots are pulled out that we can experience true freedom and deliverance—making room for the fruits of the Spirit to flourish.

My earliest recollection of lying goes back to when I was eight years old. Eager to have a cat, I told my father that I had been praying to the Lord for one. I figured that if I directly asked him for a cat, he would likely say no. Instead, I appealed to his emotions with the notion of prayer, believing he would feel more inclined to fulfill my request. A few weeks later, I got a kitten. This experience affirmed my false sinful belief that lying could sometimes lead to better results than honesty.

As a result, I fell into a cycle of deceit that persisted into adulthood, making me a habitual liar. Even when exposed, I tried to fabricate excuses. After surrendering my life to the Lord, I knew I needed to change. Lying was no longer an option. I prayed, "Holy Spirit, please convict me whenever I lie." And indeed, He did! Still, having dug myself into a deep hole, I often felt trapped. There were moments when I chose to ignore the Holy Spirit's nudging. Unfortunately, this saddened Him, and I could feel His convictions lessening within my heart. It hurt to know I was grieving the Holy Spirit.

Recognizing my need for support, I began discussing my lying habits with my therapist. She suggested strategies to help me avoid lying. While they sometimes worked, they weren't reliable. I realized that even when I didn't voice a lie, the thought would still occupy my mind, which was itself a form of deceit. "For it is from within, out of a person's heart, that evil thoughts come ...deceit ... All these evils come from inside and defile a person." (Mark 7: 21-23) Even my thoughts were defiling me before God.

I turned to the Holy Spirit, seeking His guidance. I contemplated the reasons behind my tendency to lie, and the Lord revealed the core of my struggle—lying was just a symptom. The real issue was my fear of rejection, a flaw I had inherited from my family.

My fear didn't arise from societal judgment but from the possibility of rejection by my family and church community. I observed this cultural issue reflected in my parents' lives as well. Once the Lord made this clear to me, my focus shifted back to establishing my identity in Christ. By firmly embracing who I am in Him, I could accept the possibility of rejection from others—the church, my family, and the world—similar to what Christ experienced. Grounding myself in Him, I found I had no reason for deception. His was the only acceptance I sought after.

We all fall short of God's glory. If we were flawless, we wouldn't need Him. This truth highlights the remarkable nature of His grace: the Lord wishes to heal us and free us from sin. His love transcends our imperfections. It drives Him to reach out, yearning for our restoration. He has beautiful fruits for His children to bring forth in their lives, if we allow Him to room to help us clear out the weeds. It starts by trading in your gardening shears for a spade. Then be willing to let Him dig deep, even when it hurts. Freedom is waiting just a little deeper.

Reflect on what the Lord has already liberated you from in your life. It could be a destructive habit, the burden of past mistakes, or a negative mindset, that once kept you stuck. How has that freedom changed your perspective and deepened your relationship with Him?

As we walk with God, we often come across obstacles that seem to resurface again and again. Think of a struggle you've faced— one that didn't go away no matter how many times you "cut it off" at the surface. Was there something deeper beneath the outward behavior?

Digging out the root takes more effort and intentionality, but it leads to true and lasting freedom. Write about what that process looked like for you. How was it different from simply managing the symptoms?

What did God reveal to you in that deeper place? How did His truth begin to heal the root?

Ask the Lord if there are any other roots He wants to uncover and heal today. He is gentle and faithful in every step of the journey.

_____

_____

_____

_____

_____

Dreams

He speaks in dreams, in visions of the night
when deep sleep falls on people as they lie in
their beds. He whispers in their ears and terrifies
them with warnings. He makes them turn from
doing wrong; he keeps them from pride.

JOB 33:15-17 (NIV)

WHEN ELIJAH WAS AT HIS LOWEST, God came to speak to him. He was not heard in the great wind, the earthquake, or the fire, but in a still small voice. Jehovah revealed Himself to young Joseph in the night, filling his mind with vivid visions of the future. He sent troubling dreams to plague Pharaoh's mind for His mighty will to be accomplished. Throughout history, God has spoken to people in dreams—when their minds are finally in a quiet place, their hearts are open, and their ears can hear.

I believe that God continues to communicate with us through our dreams. Since childhood, I have been a dreamer, occasionally waking with powerful memories of dreams that felt real. After I surrendered my life to Him, I noticed my dreams becoming more vivid and meaningful. In fact, the inspiration for this journal came from one of those dreams.

Dreams from God are not always as straightforward as one might hope. They often carry deeper meanings, with symbols representing various aspects of our lives. Neither Pharoah nor his advisors could understand the meaning of the lean and fat cows that tormented his sleep or the purpose behind the healthy and barren stalks of corn he saw.

At the beginning of my journey to understand my dreams, I often felt a sense of confusion. My confusion stemmed from waking up with an intense feeling, as though the Lord was warning me about something impending or drawing my attention to issues within myself that needed addressing. But without the ability to interpret these dreams, I felt I was walking in the dark, uncertain of what guidance they were meant to provide.

I prayed fervently, asking the Holy Spirit for help in understanding the message God was sending. There were times when I received clear insights, but other moments left me struggling to understand their meanings. In my search for clarity, I prayed for the Lord to send me destiny helpers—individuals like Joseph gifted in the art of dream interpretation. In response to my prayers, the Lord introduced me to a church member and dear sister, Kimberly. She had been walking with the Lord for many years and was blessed with profound revelations from Him.

We would spend countless hours on the phone, where I'd pour out my heart, sharing the vivid dreams that occupied my mind. Kimberly, with her deep understanding of divine messages, would carefully help me unpack what the Lord was revealing through each dream. I found that almost every dream I recounted addressed something fundamental within me or hinted at significant events that were yet to unfold in my life.

As our conversations deepened over the months, Kimberly began mentoring me, cultivating my ability to interpret these dreams. She taught me to be attentive to the subtle nuances of each dream, emphasizing the importance of prayer and leaning on the Holy Spirit for insight. Our discussions opened my eyes to the symbols and emotions that accompanied my dreams, helping me realize that they were not merely random images, but messages from the Lord meant to guide and instruct me.

Under her guidance and through the Holy Spirit, I gained confidence in my interpretations, gradually uncovering the layers of meaning hidden within my dreams. The process was transformative. With continued practice, I became more connected to the divine principles that govern our lives, and a sense of empowerment emerged as I learned to decode the inspirations and warnings God was showing me.

In today's fast-paced world, it is easy to dismiss dreams as insignificant or merely a byproduct of our busy minds. We often shrug them off and drift back to sleep, potentially missing out on meaningful messages from the Lord.

Dreams have the potential to offer insight, healing, and guidance. They are invitations to explore our inner worlds, confront our fears, and embrace our burdens with the assurance that we are not alone. By actively engaging with our dreams and seeking understanding, we open ourselves to a deeper relationship with the divine and allow the Lord to speak powerfully into our lives.

Once I realized that my dreams were a form of communication from the Lord, I made it a priority to keep a journal and a pen within reach of my bed. Whenever I awoke from an intense dream—regardless of the hour—I would immediately sit up and jot down every detail while it was still fresh in my mind. This simple act became a critical element in my routine.

Each entry in my journal became a window into my spiritual life, revealing insights and guidance that I might have otherwise overlooked. As I began to revisit those entries, a remarkable pattern unfolded. I noticed connections between my dreams and real-life situations, illuminating my journey and helping me navigate challenges with greater understanding. This practice unveiled the ongoing divine nudges in my daily life and fostered a heightened awareness of the spiritual realm around me.

Reflect on a time when you were given a dream by the Lord. What transpired in that dream? Was there a scene or message that stood out—something that resonated deeply within your spirit? Perhaps the dream was vivid or metaphorical, inviting you to examine certain aspects of your life or guiding you toward a particular decision.

How did this dream shape your life moving forward? Did it bring clarity, spark inspiration, or stir a call to action? Were you able to interpret its meaning, either through prayerful reflection or with the help of trusted mentors? Interpreting dreams can be both enlightening and challenging, requiring openness to the Holy Spirit's guidance. Sometimes, the meaning becomes clearer over time, revealing new layers of significance that speak to different seasons of your life.

In my own journey, I often turn back to my journal for comfort and clarity. When faced with uncertainty, rereading past dreams reminds me of the Lord's presence and guidance, even amidst challenges. These reflections became a source of encouragement and proof of His leading in every season, reinforcing my trust in His plan.

Now, take time to record: Has God ever spoken to you through a dream? What did it reveal—and how has it shaped your walk with Him?

_____

_____

_____

_____

_____

DAY 13:

Testing

How long, Lord? Will you forget me forever?
How long will you hide your face from me?

PSALM 13:1 (NIV)

EVERY SINGLE PERSON will experience a myriad of tests throughout their life. In many ways, these trials are simply part of the human experience. Since the Fall, all creation has endured hardships. For Christians, our testing is God-designed with a purpose and a plan and used for our eternal good and His ultimate glory.

In the book of Judges, we learn that although God had previously commanded the Israelites to drive out all the inhabitants of the Promised Land, He intentionally left some nations behind. These nations were meant to test Israel, to teach them warfare, and to reveal whether they would obey the Lord's commands (Judges 3:1, 4). Throughout the Old Testament, we see how these remaining nations became a constant source of trouble for Israel. The rest of Judges reads like a cycle: the Israelites did evil in the sight of the Lord, He handed them over to their enemies, they cried out for help, and God raised up a deliverer to rescue them. Again and again, they were tested—and again and again, they failed by turning to other gods.

Today, we have the Old Testament as a mirror, revealing our own nature and our deep, ongoing need for a Savior. We too will face tests—and without Him, we too will fall short.

My pastor gave a message on the well-known Psalm 23, calling it a guide for life once you submit yourself to the Lord. The chapter can be outlined in this vein as a step-by-step path for believers.

The initial verse reads, "The Lord is my shepherd; I shall not want." (KJV) When you first give your life to the Lord, He nurtures you with tender loving care. Whatever you seek, He is typically there to provide Then, "He maketh me to lie down in green pastures; He leadeth me beside the still waters." In this phase, you experience peace. Everything aligns with your hopes, and you are on a healing journey.

It continues, "He restoreth my soul." At this moment, you find yourself restored—upright and walking closely with the Lord. The chapter goes on to say, "Yea, though I walk through the valley of the shadow of death, I will fear no evil: for Thou art with me; Thy rod and Thy staff, they comfort me." This signifies a time of testing. It may feel like you are not hearing from God as you used to, but you have walked with Him long enough to know that He is always there. My pastor mentioned that this is the moment when people either push forward or fold. The shadow of death feels very much like death itself, and until we pass this test, we cannot move forward with the Lord's plan for our lives.

It's often said that the teacher is silent during the test—but that doesn't mean he's left the room. In seasons of testing, you may not hear God's voice, but that doesn't mean He's absent. God is always near;

He has promised never to leave nor forsake us. Still, there are moments when all we hear is silence—times that can make us feel forgotten or alone. In these difficult spaces, we're called to stand firm, resisting the lies and doubts planted by the enemy. Instead, we anchor ourselves in the truth of God's Word. His promises are unchanging. His presence is constant. Even when you can't feel Him, He is still with you.

Reflect on a time when you deeply needed the Lord but felt His presence was distant. Maybe it was during a personal crisis, a season of grief, or a time of uncertainty. How did you process your feelings about His silence? When God feels distant and answers don't come quickly, it's easy to grow discouraged—yet it's in those quiet places that our faith is stretched and strengthened.

What did you do in that season? Did you search the Scriptures for comfort or pour your heart out in prayer? Perhaps you leaned on the encouragement of others or simply held on, even when it was difficult to understand what God was doing.

Looking back, what did you learn? Often, these waiting seasons become sacred ground where perseverance, trust, and spiritual maturity take root. Standing firm in faith during silence strengthens our ability to recognize God's character amid life's trials.

Let this be a space to explore how God may have been working, even when it was hard to see.

Witness

Therefore go and make disciples of all
nations, baptizing them in the name of the
Father and of the Son and of the Holy Spirit,
and teaching them to obey everything I have
commanded you. And teaching them to obey
everything I have commanded you.

◡ MATTHEW 28:19-20 [NIV]

JESUS LEFT HIS FOLLOWERS WITH the responsibility to reflect His light to
this dark world and spread the Gospel throughout the earth. In word.
In action. Always with love. This is the great commission. Yet it is eas-
ier said than done. When faced with the opportunity, do we share the
truth of our Savior? Or do we falter, stumbling over worries about how
the hearer will receive it? Missing that chance to share the Gospel can
result in long term regret.

As a young teen, I had an experience I would never forget. Enveloped in the warmth of a church service heavy with worship, I felt the spirit of the Lord surround me, and I collapsed to the floor. What ensued was both surreal and frightening. I was thrust into a pitch-black space—so dark that words can't capture its intensity. Suspended in that void, I realized with unease that I was in a place that wasn't mine. The darkness clung to me, suffocating like a shroud, as anguished voices erupted from below.

"It's your fault! Why didn't you tell me?" Their harsh accusations sliced through the air. Each word pierced my spirit as I trembled and wept in despair. Unable to defend myself, an overwhelming sense of guilt consumed me. My parents watched helplessly as I remained unresponsive, my eyes shut tightly against the scene I had fallen into. In that dark space, one voice cut through the chaos—a woman's voice, sharp and unforgiving. Her cruel words echoed in the void, deepening my feelings of worthlessness as she unleashed a stream of hurtful charges against me.

In a jolt of consciousness, I was back, lying in the rear of my parents' minivan with my head gently resting in my mother's lap. The comfort of her presence was soothing, yet the lingering fear clung to me like a shadow.

Concern etched across her face, my mother asked in a quivering voice, "What happened?" The weight of my recent experience crashed over me once more. I recounted my journey through that dark place—the voices, the overwhelming despair—and everything felt surreal as I spoke. Disbelief washed over her features, as if the gravity of my story was too much to bear. Time passed, and gradually, the intense experience began to fade from memory. Like any thirteen-year-old, I returned to my life, occupied with the usual adolescent concerns—school, friends, dreams, and daily anxieties—pushing aside the terror and confusion that had briefly engulfed me.

Nearly eighteen years later, I would encounter a situation that would bring the haunting experience into my real life. I had found solace in an unexpected friendship with a woman named Tina at work. Tina was full of life, yet she had encountered her own struggles. Since she didn't drive, I frequently gave her rides to and from work. These trips turned into treasured moments for us both. Some evenings, we would hang out in the car, her cigarette smoke spiraling softly into the air as we shared meaningful conversations.

Her story captivated me. Tina was raised in a devout Hindu household by Indian parents and defied her family's expectations by choosing a love marriage—something strictly forbidden in her culture. As a result, she was completely shunned, left to face life's challenges on her own. Her journey became even more difficult when tragedy struck: her husband passed away, leaving her to raise their young daughter alone in an increasingly isolating world.

She shared an apartment with her male cousin, who seemed somewhat odd to me. I sensed a discomfort about him, but I never addressed it with Tina then. Instead, I aimed to be supportive during our talks, lending an ear to her struggles and successes. In those moments together, her strong character illuminated our connection, forging a bond that went beyond our different backgrounds.

Although I disliked Tina's smoking, I had come to accept her right to indulge in it. Our talks brought warmth, and for a while, I embraced this habit as part of her identity. One day out of concern, I chose to address it. "Tina," I said softly, "I think you should think about quitting. I want you to have a long life." Her reply surprised me. "I don't drink. I don't party. All I do is work and care for my daughter. This is the only thing I enjoy," she said firmly. "I need this for myself."

Her words resonated deeply within me, sparking a conviction that was both unfamiliar and alluring. In that instant, a quiet inner voice encouraged me to share my past faith in the Lord with her. I was surprised, as I hadn't been following Him since I was nineteen. The idea felt disingenuous. Stuck in this internal conflict, I pushed the thought aside, brushing off the urge as we went about our day. Still, I couldn't ignore the understanding that behind her tough exterior lay a yearning for connection, maybe even a wish for something more profound.

Throughout the months, her cousin would often come to pick her up after work. Each time, I would wave at him across the parking lot, trying to push past my uncomfortable impression of him. Yet, his reaction was always the same: he would look my way briefly before turning away, never acknowledging my wave. I mentioned it once to Tina, asking if he was alright.

"That's just who he is," she answered, a trace of annoyance in her tone. "Just ignore him."

While I honored her wishes, I couldn't shake the unease about her living situation. Her cousin's behavior raised concerns, creating a subtle tension as I grappled with the complexities of her life. Even during our warm conversations, an underlying unease lurked, reminding me that her world wasn't as straightforward as it appeared. A year later, I reached a significant milestone and purchased my first home. The exhilaration of leaving behind my shared living arrangement—three roommates and two kids all competing for a single bathroom—was thrilling. I was excited to embrace the independence that came with having a space I could genuinely call my own.

A few weeks after settling in, Tina came to me with an unexpected request. "Would it be possible for my daughter and me to stay with you for a while?" she asked, her eyes reflecting a mix of hope and uncertainty. I hesitated and gently asked why she needed to move in, but she didn't offer any specific reason. Her vagueness made me uneasy. Thinking of my own comfort, I selfishly asked for some time to adjust and told her I'd let her know later.

At that moment, I felt conflicted. The idea of opening my newly found sanctuary felt overwhelming, but I couldn't overlook the needs of my friend, who had already endured so many hardships. While I dealt with my mixed feelings of excitement and anxiety about my new home, I struggled with the decision that hung heavily over me. Surprisingly, Tina never mentioned her request again. Months had passed since I settled into my new place, and my life became increasingly hectic. I got a promotion at work, which occupied most of my time and caused me to visit Tina less often. I frequently thought about her but didn't reach out, believing I could reconnect once things calmed down.

One fateful day at work, I received devastating news that changed everything. Tina had been killed in what authorities labeled as a homicide-suicide. Her cousin had taken her life with a hammer before taking his own. The impact of this tragedy overwhelmed me, and I was left with a heavy heart filled with grief and regret. In the days and months that followed, I sank into a deep depression. The burden of my guilt felt unending. I turned to alcohol, desperately attempting to numb the pain and shame from knowing I could have helped her. I came to the painful realization that when she needed support, I chose not to extend a lifeline when I had the opportunity. Surrounded by alcohol and sadness, I wrestled with memories of our talks. I questioned whether my hesitation could have altered her life's path. Every thought pierced my heart like a dagger, plunging me further into despair.

Six years later, I rediscovered my purpose by dedicating my life to the Lord. One evening, while praying and meditating for comfort and direction, I was unexpectedly drawn back into that haunting darkness. The familiar screams surrounded me, breaking the silence as accusing voices cried out, "It's your fault! Why didn't you tell me?"

Once again, amidst the chaos, a woman's voice cut through the noise—a voice that sparked both dread and recognition. It was Tina. The warmth that once characterized our conversations now gave way to the heaviness of unresolved grief and unspoken questions. "Why didn't you tell me?" Her words resonated with deep sorrow.

In that moment, I faced the stark reality of my past decisions, coming to grips with how many chances I had missed to reach out and offer the support she needed. But even more importantly, I felt a deep regret that I hadn't shared the one thing that could have given her hope—the saving knowledge of the Lord. This heavy realization intensified my feelings of failure. It was as though I held the key to a door that could have offered her solace and strength, yet I chose to keep it locked, leaving her in darkness while she yearned for light.

Sharing the Good News of the Lord is both nerve-wracking and exhilarating. On one side, fear can seize you as you fret about being judged or misunderstood, making you hesitate to leave your comfort zone. The idea of discussing your faith with someone may evoke doubts over whether your words will be accepted. Conversely, there's a palpable excitement stemming from your own journey of freedom and transformation—a deep desire to share that hope and joy with others. This distinct contrast creates a complex web of emotions, where fear mingles with a fervent wish to spread the light that has guided your own journey.

You are created to be a light to this world, reflecting the goodness and glory of Christ. Shine brightly, so others can be drawn to Him.

Reflect on a time when you had the privilege of sharing the Good News with someone who then gave their life to the Lord. What happened at that moment? What words did you choose, and how did the conversation unfold? Was it spontaneous, or did it feel like a divine appointment orchestrated by God? Perhaps you shared your personal testimony—how His grace transformed your life—or maybe you spoke directly from Scripture, letting God's promises speak for themselves.

The Bible tells us that heaven rejoices when a soul is saved. What a beautiful reminder that each salvation experience is cause for celebration. Think about how you felt in that moment when you witnessed the joy their eyes or the peace settle over them as they accepted Christ. What part of that moment reminded you of God's incredible love and the power of the Gospel?

If you haven't yet had the chance to share your faith, think back to a time when someone shared theirs with you. What impact did it have on your life? Then, write down a few Scriptures and a prayer asking God to prepare your heart for the next opportunity He gives you to share His truth with someone in need.

Pray

This is the confidence we have in approaching God: that if we ask anything according to his will, he hears us. And if we know that he hears us—whatever we ask—we know that we have what we asked of him.

○ 1 JOHN 5:14-15 (NIV)

PRAYER IS POWERFUL. Prayer changes things. Jesus told His disciples if they had faith merely the size of a tiny mustard seed, they could say to a mountain "be moved" and it would be so. Countless scriptures tell us to call on God and assure us that He will answer. Yet there's that key phrase from the scripture in I John—if we ask according to His will. While God is fully able to do anything, His will is immutable. Unchanging. We must first align ourselves with the Father—an important lesson I had yet to learn before this experience.

One day, I penned a prayer in my journal. "Father God, I am so grateful for the love and joy You've imparted to me. I cherish Your unconditional love, even in moments when I feel unworthy. Thank You for always being by my side, even when I have trouble feeling Your presence. Father, you remind us to lay our burdens at Your feet because You care for us. Right now, I am feeling overwhelmed. My financial obligations are weighing heavily on me, and I humbly seek Your assistance. I have bought over twenty lottery tickets because I sincerely believe You can help me win. It doesn't need to be the jackpot; I just need enough to get out of this difficult situation. Father, I know You are capable of all things, so I trust that this request is not too much for You. Please, Papa, lend me Your help! Your loving daughter."

When I woke up the next day and checked my lottery tickets, the reality hit me hard—I hadn't won a single dollar. In my despair, I turned to my mother and asked, "Why didn't the Lord help me?" Her matter-of-fact response jarred me. "God isn't going to help you win the lottery because it doesn't align with the Word of God."

At the time, I didn't fully grasp the depth of her statement and felt only disappointed and confused. However, as time passed and I gained more life experience, I began to understand the wisdom behind her words. The lottery, despite my hopes, wasn't the solution to my struggles. It became clear that God's blessings often come in forms that align with His greater plan for our lives. His ways are rooted in faith, hard work, and resilience.

Using Scripture helped me connect with His promises and pray for things attuned to His purpose for my life. Instead of asking the Lord to help me win the lottery, I shifted how I approached the throne of grace. After this experience, I declared, "Father, I believe through Your promises that You have called me to lend to nations, not to borrow (Deut. 15:6). Therefore, I ask You to bless me, Lord, and expand my territories (1 Chron. 4:10), so that Your blessings may flow not just through me but to future generations as well (Psalm 115:12)." By reframing my requests through the lens of His Word, I experienced a profound shift in my heart and spirit.

This approach not only reinforced my faith but also enhanced my understanding of God's enduring wish to bless and empower me for His kingdom work. Through these scriptural affirmations, I found a deeper connection to His will and the assurance that He would provide in line with His purpose. When praying, God wants you to speak from the heart, as that is where He truly engages during your conversations with Him. It's in these genuine moments of vulnerability and sincerity that our relationship with Him strengthens. Carrying the Word of God within you enables you to embody His truths, transforming your prayers into potent declarations. When you converse with Him, you're not just repeating words; you're visualizing those words and believing in their truth, inviting His presence into every part of your life.

Here are some practical examples. You can pray over your marriage with words of life like, "Lord, keep us united in love and purpose, letting nothing and no one separate what You have joined together (Mark 10:9)." During difficult times, David's Psalms are prayers poured out on paper. Use his words intermingled with your own. When faced with a serious decision, you could pray, "God, You have promised wisdom to anyone who has asked. (James 1:5) I ask you now to fill my mind with Your wisdom that I lean not on my own understanding (Proverbs 3:5)." The scriptures are so much more than ancient words on a page. They bring light and life to all who believe. Aligning ourselves with God's will and praying His Word ensures we keep Him at the very focal point of our everyday lives.

Reflect on a time when your prayers aligned to God's Word. Can you recall a moment when you turned to Scripture during a challenging situation and found promises that shaped your prayers? As you poured your heart out, did you feel a stirring within, a deep-seated assurance that your petitions were rooted in biblical truth?

What happened next? Did you experience a breakthrough—a shift in circumstances, relationships, or your own heart? Or perhaps the outcome wasn't what you expected. Did the Lord respond in a different way—through peace, wisdom, or a redirection that revealed His greater plan?

Consider a time when God's answer was "no" or "wait." How did that shape your understanding of His will? What did you learn about trust, timing, and surrender? Sometimes, His greatest answers come in forms we do not immediately recognize. He may have provided comfort, peace, or guidance that wasn't aligned with your initial request but was precisely what you needed.

Whether or not your prayers were answered as hoped, how did the experience grow and shape your faith? Did it deepen your trust in His sovereignty and goodness, reminding you that He sees the bigger picture?

These moments remind us that prayer isn't just about outcomes—it's about drawing closer to God. When we pray His Word and stay open to His guidance, our hearts are transformed, and our connection with Him deepens.

Protection

The Lord will keep you from all harm— he will watch over your life; the Lord will watch over your coming and going both now and forevermore.

PSALM 121:7-8 [NIV]

WHEREVER WE GO AND WHATEVER WE DO, our lives are never hidden from God. David declared that even in the womb, he was fully known by the Lord (Psalm 139:15–16). Paul reminded the church in Ephesus that God chose us in Christ before the foundation of the world (Ephesians 1:4). The Creator's knowledge of His creation is intimate and intricate, and His care for it is both intentional and immaculate.

In my testimony about surrendering my life to the Lord, I've often shared how I wandered for seventeen years. While this is accurate, He was always by my side. Even when I didn't serve Him, God's hand was ever present in my life. I am deeply thankful for my prayerful parents, who continually supported me while I felt lost in the world. As I look back on those years, I can pinpoint crucial moments when the Lord's presence guided and safeguarded me.

When I was in my mid-thirties, a close friend eagerly wanted to introduce me to another friend of hers, whom she referred to as a seer. We planned to pick him up for a casual outing and drinks, but my friend shared something that piqued my interest: he had once read her palm, and what he predicted had indeed come true. While I was curious about the details of her experience, the thought of having my palm read made me hesitant.

Growing up, I learned that those who claim to predict the future without being connected to God are often swayed by unholy forces. I believed then and still believe now that engaging in these practices could lead to harmful consequences in my life. Still, I let my friend share her excitement as we drove to pick him up. We neared his home, and he started walking towards us. When our eyes met, I felt an uneasy sensation in the pit of my stomach. The moment he got into the car, that discomfort morphed into an overwhelming wave of pure anxiety.

I inexplicably knew something was off. When my friend introduced us, she looked at him eagerly and exclaimed, "You're going to read her palm!" In that instant, I heard an inner voice—which I now know was the Holy Spirit—warning me, "Don't let him touch you." This unexpected guidance led me to blurt out, "No, no, no! No, thank you. I don't want to know my future, and I don't engage in that." My friend kept asking why and urged me to reconsider throughout the night. Despite her encouragement, that uneasy feeling served as a constant reminder to stay resolute in my choice. Strengthened by the Father, that resolve protected me that night.

After I dedicated my life to the Lord, this memory came back to me. The Lord showed me that had I allowed that seer to read my palm, chaos and catastrophe would have consumed my life. In that reflective moment, I knelt in gratitude and thanked the Lord for shielding me from harm, even when I felt unworthy.

Jesus outlined the Father's profound care and attention to us in Matthew 10. The Lord knows when even a sparrow falls. We are worth far more than a sparrow to Him. He sees every danger that lies ahead and prepares a safe path—if we will heed His voice. Whether you've been walking with God for years or have just opened your heart to Him, understand that God has always been with you. Before we fully understand our relationship with God, we may often attribute these feelings to intuition—gut feelings warning us of danger or prompting us to make certain decisions. Yet, as our spiritual awareness grows, we realize that what we once called instinct is in fact our spirit responding to the Holy Spirit's whisperings and warnings.

His presence is a constant in our lives, often appearing in ways we might not instantly notice. We must recognize and share God's faithfulness, continually acknowledging His grace and mercy as foundational to our spiritual journeys.

Think back to a moment when you sensed God's presence, guidance, or protection in a powerful way. What was happening during that time? How did you recognize that the Lord was leading you?

Perhaps you found yourself in a situation that didn't feel quite right, and you felt a nudge to take a different path or pause before making a choice. Did you follow that prompting? In hindsight, how might God have been steering you toward protection, wisdom, or blessing?

Reflect on how these experiences have deepened your awareness of God's intricate involvement in your life and the importance of being attuned to His voice. Conversely, if you ignore that nudge, take a moment to consider the consequences. What patterns have you noticed in how He communicates with you? How can you continue cultivating a heart that hears Him clearly in the future? Recognizing these instances allows us to appreciate God's continual presence and desire to protect and guide us through life's complexities.

DAY 17:

Choice

You intended to harm me, but God intended it for good to accomplish what is now being done, the saving of many lives.

⌁ GENESIS 50:20 [NIV]

WHILE GOD'S PROTECTION IS REAL, He is also our Heavenly Father. Like any good father, He allows His children to make choices and experience the consequences. Every choice we make creates a ripple effect, and sadly, giving our lives to the Lord doesn't protect us from the repercussions of poor decisions. "Because the Lord disciplines the one He loves, and He chastens everyone He accepts as His son" (Heb. 12:6). Experiencing the effects—even the painful ones—of our decisions helps us grow in our Christian maturity. God guides us in every situation, especially through our mistakes.

Prior to my commitment to the Lord, I started a business venture that I thought would enhance life for my family and me. Before jumping fully in, God warned me countless times, but I opted to ignore those signs.

I recognized that starting a business would be challenging and reminded myself that if it were easy, everyone would do it. When I faced the hurdle of limited funds, I didn't give up; instead, I looked for other options. Even when I partnered with people whose integrity I later doubted, I dismissed my worries. Aware that my job might not approve of my new endeavor, I kept everything under wraps. I even sought a prophetic word to ease my anxiety and instead received a warning about potential legal troubles. When I was given the chance to stop and heed that admonition, instead I forged ahead.

My business partner was also my closest friend and, when she decided to leave our venture, I felt both angry and determined to prove her wrong. I had many chances to walk away, but I chose to stay. However, the business failed, resulting in a heavy burden of debt.

This experience had its purpose, as every situation in life does. Like the prodigal son. this painful financial failure turned me back to the Father.

How can we determine if God is guiding us or if the Enemy is leading us astray? When we feel led in a certain direction and encounter roadblocks, is it the Holy Spirit giving a warning or the enemy trying to discourage and interfere? After committing my life to the Lord, I felt peace, even in the face of the significant debt that had previously kept me awake countless nights. Profound calm replaced my anxiety. God frequently encourages us to take actions that stretch our comfort zones and test our limits. Yet, there should ultimately be a sense of peace in our hearts.

The decisions we make throughout our lives can have lasting impacts, shaping our present and influencing our future. Each choice, no matter how minor, adds to the intricate fabric of our journey. I find comfort in the profound truth revealed in Joseph's story: what the Enemy intends for harm, God can always transform for good. This assurance brings hope, reminding us that regardless of our past choices, redemption and transformation are always attainable.

Think about a time when you were faced with a significant decision. Was there a certain moment when you sensed God prompting you to choose a different path—perhaps walk away from a toxic relationship, pursue a new career, or take steps more aligned with His purpose for your life? How did the Holy Spirit speak to you, and did you heed the gentle nudging?

If you followed His guidance, how did that decision manifest in your life? Perhaps it opened doors you never anticipated, leading you to new opportunities, deeper relationships, or profound personal growth. Obedience often creates ripples of blessing that extend far beyond the initial moment of decision.

Conversely, if you resisted that prompt, what happened next? Did it lead to a period of struggle, regret, or distance from the Lord? What did you learn through that process?

Finally, how has this shaped your ability to recognize and respond to His voice today? What would you do differently now?

Remember, it's essential to approach these reflections with grace. Each choice serves as a stepping stone on your spiritual journey. Even if some decisions led to hardship, God is capable of weaving those experiences into something beautiful. The challenges we face can cultivate resilience and ultimately deepen our faith, providing us with insights that shape who we become.

_____

_____

_____

_____

Deep Wounds

**Be kind and compassionate to one another,
forgiving each other, just as in Christ God forgave you.**

EPHESIANS 4:32 (NIV)

WHILE WE'VE ALREADY had a chapter on forgiveness, it's a topic necessary to revisit often throughout the entirety of our lives. There will always be another hurt, another grievance, another wrongdoing. With Jesus' command to forgive the same person repeatedly, there's no question that forgiveness will forever be part of our stories here on earth. Yet, there are some wounds that run far deeper than a thoughtless word or gesture. These are papercuts compared to the gaping trauma many have endured.

During the early phases of my faith journey, I understood that forgiveness is an active choice that fosters true healing and liberation. Then my belief was put to the test as God began to unveil memories

I had pushed aside, allowing me to face the pain and trauma from my childhood. Acknowledging the scars was my first step towards reconciliation—not just with those who had caused me pain, but also with myself. Unearthing my past was challenging. Like peeling an onion, each layer exposed deeper, lingering wounds in need of healing. I realized that clinging to grief and anger was a heavy load that prevented me from fully experiencing God's love.

As I prayed, I asked the Lord for understanding and clarity, unaware of the true origins of my pain. One night, feeling particularly vulnerable, I drifted off to sleep and was abruptly drawn back to a buried childhood memory from when I was just three years old, feeling confused and frightened. The details of my uncle sexually assaulting me came rushing back with remarkable clarity, bearing a heavy emotional impact. At that moment, the Lord not only disclosed the events that took place but also illuminated the state of my heart.

I came to understand that my difficulties with forgiveness were not limited to my predator; I also carried significant resentment toward my parents. I believed that they should have protected me, but instead, they overlooked my trauma, opting to hide it away. This historically societal norm of silence surrounding complex topics made it even harder for me to express my pain and find the healing I so urgently needed.

In many cultures, discussing issues like abuse is often seen as taboo. Families prioritize reputation and harmony over confronting the hidden struggles beneath the surface. Initially, I thought that simply saying, "I forgive them, Father. I just want to move on," would free me from the emotional burdens that weighed me down. Yet, despite my genuine attempts, I felt persistent emptiness inside. I soon came to understand that forgiveness is a continuous and deep process demanding more than mere words; it requires a heartfelt exploration of my feelings and experiences. With a strong desire to progress, I started conversations with my family.

I reached out to my mother, father, sister, and therapist one by one. I needed to truly grasp what transpired during those formative years, not only to forgive but to express my truth. Each dialogue became crucial in my quest for authenticity and genuine forgiveness. Speaking with my parents, who also carried hurts and fears, helped me uncover layers of generational pain. I wrestled with my judgments and beliefs as a mother and an adult. While I wanted to hold them accountable for what I considered their failures, I also began to recognize them as individuals influenced by their own traumas and cultural backgrounds. It became clear to me that they, too, were part of a generational cycle in which hurt people often inflict pain on others.

This realization illuminated the fact that they might have lacked the tools or knowledge to shield me from harm. I developed compassion for their limitations, recognizing they were dealing with a story they had inherited. While this understanding doesn't justify their actions, it enabled me to acknowledge their humanity and the challenges they encountered.

Although I've made considerable progress in forgiving, I can't say the struggle has ended. Every day brings new challenges, and I frequently encounter internal conflicts. Sometimes, I quietly say, "Lord, help me." Forgiveness is not just a one-time statement but an ongoing process.

Reflecting on my journey, I was deeply moved to ask myself this question. How can I seek the Lord's forgiveness for my repeated mistakes if I find it difficult to show that same grace to my loved ones? This feels particularly poignant, considering Matthew 6:14-15: "For if you forgive other people when they offend you, your heavenly Father will also forgive you. But if you do not forgive others their sins, your Father will not forgive your sins."

This scripture urges me to face the foundation of my beliefs regarding forgiveness. It prompts me to recognize that refusing to forgive can hinder not only my connections with others but my relationship with God. I reflect on my shortcomings and realize that, in my times of weakness, I have often repeated the behaviors of those who have caused me pain. Hurt people tend to hurt others, and I grapple with this truth as I pursue my journey of forgiveness.

In challenging times, when memories flood back or emotions become overwhelming, I remind myself of the significance of grace—not only for others but for myself too. Setbacks are acceptable as long as I stay dedicated to my journey. Every prayer for help and each moment of reflection serves as a step towards healing. When I think about my past—my relationships with family and friends—I can't ignore the betrayals and deceptions that almost extinguished my ability to love. These experiences often felt like dark clouds overshadowing my heart, making me doubt my faith in people. However, as my relationship with the Lord grew more substantial, I came to a pivotal realization: I cannot genuinely love God without extending that love to His people. The bond we share is deeply interconnected, mirroring the very essence of God's love for us.

Recall a moment when you felt the Lord urging you to forgive—whether someone else or yourself. What made it difficult? Perhaps anger or betrayal clouded your ability to let go, or you feared that forgiveness might be mistaken for approval of what was done. Did you wrestle with releasing the past?

Now think about the moments when healing began. When did you feel the gentle encouragement of the Holy Spirit nudging you toward forgiveness? Did you find solace in prayer, seeking God's guidance as you navigated your feelings? Maybe you came to see how holding on to resentment weighed you down more than you realized. What shifted in you—what moment revealed that forgiveness had taken root?

Forgiveness often brings a sense of release, a lightness where heavy bitterness once resided. Perhaps your heart moved from resentment to compassion, indicating that you were aligning with God's heart. He restores that which is broken.

In the end, remember that forgiveness is a journey, not a destination. It involves ongoing growth and reliance on God's grace. Every moment of release draws you closer to God's heart—where wholeness, not hurt, has the final word.

Thanksgiving

**Rejoice always, pray continually,
give thanks in all circumstances;
this is God's will for you in Christ Jesus.**

⌒ 1 THESSALONIANS 5:16-18 [NIV]

THE INSTRUCTION IN THIS SCRIPTURE is a joyful command when we're standing on the mountaintop—celebrating victories and clearly seeing God's hand at work. But the command remains the same in the valley, even when the skies grow dark and heavy, and God seems silent in our hour of need. Yes, even then, we are called to give thanks and rejoice. In both our highest and lowest moments, He is present. No matter our circumstances, He remains worthy of our praise and thanksgiving. In every season—He is still God.

Going through my previous journal entries has been quite enlightening. I saw how often I complained and requested more during challenging times. Every obstacle made me question the Lord as I constantly struggled with my circumstances. I knew this journey wouldn't be simple, yet I frequently turned my attention to my complaints instead of recognizing the lessons revealed.

This season of my life is dedicated to celebrating the goodness of the Lord and expressing my heartfelt appreciation for Him. I frequently forget that although I may feel distanced from God in times of struggle, He has never left my side. When loneliness creeps in, I recognize it is a trick of the enemy designed to make me believe that the Lord has abandoned me. The truth is that He never leaves us; He never forsakes us. He is always there, even when we can't perceive His presence.

Thank You, Father. As I look back over the time since I dedicated my life to You, I am in awe of everything I've faced. There were moments when I questioned my ability to overcome my obstacles, but my own strength never saw me through. It was You. You were my sustenance. You provided me with strength. You blessed me with your eternal peace that transcends all understanding. For that, I am deeply thankful. I appreciate the well-being of my family and my health. I am grateful for the roof over my head, the food that nourishes me, and the love that fills my heart.

I am grateful for your constant love and support through life's challenges, and most importantly for Your repeated forgiveness. Thank You for Your mercy and grace which offer me shelter during uncertain and fearful times. Lord, I appreciate everything You are and all that You continue to do in my life. My gratitude is everlasting.

The Psalms are the perfect example of how we can go through valleys and even struggle with dark thoughts yet still end with prayer and thanksgiving. Time and time again we see David call upon the Lord, questioning Him over what He is doing and why He's allowing his enemies to seemingly find victory. But David always included a "yet" in these prayers from his heart: Yet will I praise Him. Yet will I trust

Him. Yet will I worship Him. Whether you're in your mountaintop experience or struggling through the valley, it's alright to cry out to God. He's fully capable of handling our doubts and fears. But always return to your "yet," thanking and praising Him anyway.

In seasons of struggle, it's easy to focus on our disappointment and overlook His presence. Even as we pray for help, we may miss the quiet ways He is already sustaining us. Take a moment to reflect on the blessings that surround you—both the obvious and the overlooked. From the rising sun to the kindness of a friend, from the strength that carries you through pain to the peace that calms your spirit, each is a reminder of His love and faithfulness.

What stirs gratitude in your heart today? Recall moments when you sensed His guidance or comfort during tough times. Let those memories remind you that even in the midst of hardship, God is near.

Cultivating a habit of thankfulness shifts our focus and renews our spirit. Begin each day by thanking the Lord for who He is and what He's done. As gratitude takes root, you'll begin to see His hand more clearly—in every circumstance, every moment.

Deliverance

For he has rescued us from the dominion of darkness and brought us into the kingdom of the Son he loves, in whom we have redemption, the forgiveness of sins.

COLOSSIANS 1:13-14(NIV)

JESUS CASTED OUT MANY DEMONS during his ministry, and the apostles carried on that work after His ascension. The scripture makes it clear that our greatest struggles are not against flesh and blood, but against powers of darkness and spiritual forces of evil. As His children, we may fall under oppression of spiritual darkness, but we are promised deliverance in Christ.

Being part of a church that embraced the move of the Spirit, deliverance was essential to community life. Services are often dynamic, filled with passionate worship and the unmistakable presence of God. At times, individuals with gentle voices suddenly burst into screams or powerful shouts; their voices became almost unrecognizable.

Often deliverance would appear more dramatic, with individuals visually manifesting during the service. The preacher, inspired by the Holy Spirit and following Jesus' example would command the spirit within them to depart using authoritative yet compassionate language.

After deliverance occurred, something extraordinary would unfold. Individuals would revert to their previous selves, their expressions becoming gentle as if God had removed a significant weight. They frequently had little or no memory of the events during that pivotal moment. Such experiences of deliverance frequently occurred among believers who had participated in multiple services yet only recently started to reveal the evil spirits within them. As someone still navigating this journey, I often pondered my own path. I thought, "I've spent seventeen years without the Lord in my heart. It's clear that I need deliverance."

Every time the preacher was inspired to call for demons to reveal themselves, I tensed up, sure that I would also show signs. I truly felt that something inside me required attention. To my astonishment, nothing transpired. Week after week, service after service, I waited eagerly, but no manifestation occurred.

In my pursuit of freedom, I began following a preacher online who guided viewers through self-deliverance techniques. I carefully implemented the steps he provided, aspiring for a breakthrough. Despite my efforts, I found myself questioning why I hadn't experienced the same results that others had.

This prompted a period of reflection for me. I started to question both the state of my soul and the very concept of deliverance. I understood that although deliverance is a significant part of the Christian journey, its expression varies from person to person. Everyone's relationship with the Lord is unique and characterized by distinct challenges and victories. Through my engagement with the community and my quest for understanding, I realized that deliverance is not just a singular event but an ongoing process. It encompasses continual healing, personal growth, and a closer connection with God. God reaches us in our current state, working within our hearts and lives in ways that might not always be apparent or immediate.

What I learned from this experience was that my path to liberation might have looked different than others, but it was no less valid. Ultimately, deliverance is about allowing God to work in us—purging the influences that hinder our walk with Him and leading us toward spiritual wholeness. The outward manifestation of deliverance is just the tip of the iceberg, often representing a much deeper transformation taking place within. Whether we have that casting out event or not, we can each put on the full armor of God and take our stand against the devil's schemes every single day, in His strength and with His help.

Reflect on a time when you needed deliverance. How was that revealed to you? Perhaps it emerged during a moment of prayer when the Holy Spirit surfaced a burden you had been carrying for too long. Or maybe it became clear through a series of events that exposed patterns of fear, sin, or emotional heaviness.

What were you seeking freedom from? Was it a recurring struggle, an unhealthy relationship, anxiety, or a sense of hopelessness? These weights can drag heavily on our spirits and obstruct our ability to fully engage with God and His calling for our lives. In some cases, deliverance may come through community support—wise counsel from a trusted friend, mentor, or spiritual leader who helped you navigate your journey. God often uses the body of Christ to play a vital role in fostering healing, as sharing our burdens with others can significantly lighten the load of our struggles.

Think about how God met you in that moment. What did the process of deliverance look like for you? How did it change your view of His power and love? Write about what freedom felt like— and how you continue to walk in it today.

DAY 21:

Lessons

**Do not conform to the pattern of this world, but
be transformed by the renewing of your mind.
Then you will be able to test and approve what
God's will is—his good, pleasing, and perfect will.**

— ROMANS 12:2 (NIV)

WE WERE CREATED in the very image of God. We should be a perfect reflection of His goodness, mercy, righteousness, and love. Yet that image was marred by sin in the garden when Eve and then Adam made a choice that would ripple down to every generation thereafter. When we come to Christ, our hearts begin to long for that image to be restored.

"Lord! Fill me with your unconditional love. Guide me to love others as you love me. Let my heart long for your people and grant me the patience to support them."

This was the prayer I brought before the Lord for months—asking Him to transform the love within me so I could reflect it more fully to those around me. Though I had always tried to be kind, I began to see the limits of my willingness to be inconvenienced for others. I came to realize that true love requires sacrifice—a consistent choice to place the needs of others above my own comfort. Deep down, I recognized that my love was often conditional, and my patience was quick to fade. This not only affected my relationships but also shaped how I responded to life's daily challenges.

In my innocence, I prayed for the Lord's guidance in perfect love and patience, believing He would ignite a holy spark within me and miraculously fill my heart with these virtues. In God's immaculate wisdom, He did not answer my request as I had hoped, and I quickly discovered that His methods are much deeper and more complex than I had in mind. Instead of an immediate burst of enlightenment, He placed me in circumstances that forced me to make the choice between responding with love or surrendering to my selfish instincts. I found myself facing daily situations in which my patience was tested. I endured long grocery lines and dealt with disagreements among loved ones. Each moment became a challenge, presenting me with the choice to be selfless or give in to my urges.

The lessons I encountered were often challenging. There were moments when I faltered, responding with frustration rather than grace. Similarly, I found that my desires were not always fulfilled. Instead, I was encouraged to cultivate the virtue of patience, learning to trust in God's timing and purpose.

What became evident to me is that the Lord does answer our prayers, though often in unexpected ways. He has been chiseling away at my rough edges, molding my character through these trials much like a sculptor, turning an unsightly stone into something beautiful. Here's the kicker: God will present the same test repeatedly, dressed in different scenarios, until you pass it. It's a humbling realization that this journey of growth is ongoing, but each trial is an opportunity to embody the love and patience I've been praying for.

While the process may feel daunting at times, it is a path toward true transformation that is reworking my heart to reflect Christ's love. We often pour out prayers to God, feeling dismayed when the answers don't match our expectations. In waiting or silence, we may question if our prayers are heard. By stepping back, as I did with my prayers for love and patience, I discovered He was always answering in His way and time.

This shift in perspective can be transformative. Instead of fixating on immediate results, I learned to notice how God subtly influences our lives, which often goes unnoticed amid distractions. Paying closer attention revealed small affirmations indicating His presence.

Reflect on your own experiences with answered and unanswered prayers. What prayers have you brought before the Lord—quiet hopes, desperate cries, or steady petitions over time? Each one matters, and none goes unnoticed by Him.

How did God respond? Sometimes His answers come swiftly, offering peace or direction when we need it most. Other times, the response unfolds slowly, or not in the way we had hoped. Have you ever experienced clarity that emerged only after a long season of silence? Did He provide peace in turmoil or guide you toward a path?

Sometimes, the greatest lessons and deepest growth are hidden within these unanswered prayers. In hindsight, how did those experiences shape your understanding of God's timing and purpose?

As you journal, ask yourself: Have these lessons deepened your trust in the Lord? Have they taught you to lean not on your own understanding but on His infinite wisdom and love? Use this time to reflect on how these experiences—regardless of outcome—has drawn you closer to His heart.

Favor

Let love and faithfulness never leave you; bind them around your neck, write them on the tablet of your heart. Then you will win favor and a good name in the sight of God and man.

PROVERBS 3:3-4 (NIV)

THERE ARE TWO KINDS OF FAVOR: the favor of God and the favor of man. Both are important because, while having the favor of God is essential, it is also important to have a favorable reputation with man. This is because God's blessings often come through other people. If you possess the favor of God but lack the favor of man, those who are in a position to help you may choose not to act on your behalf due to their free will. Cultivating relationships and seeking the goodwill of others can be vital for realizing the blessings intended for us.

We see this in the story of Joseph. Clearly, he had the favor of God on his life from his youth. He began to have vivid dreams illustrating the extraordinary plan God had for his future. On the other hand, a lack of positive relationships with his brothers bred jealousy and bitterness that resulted in him being sold into slavery. While this was all a part of God's ultimate plan, it is also clear that God used the incredible experience to teach him the importance of earning his place among men too. In the prison, he won the jailer's respect to the point of being placed over the other prisoners. This path led him to his place of ultimate favor with Pharoah as his right-hand man after he interpreted the prophetic dreams of Egypt's ruler. From there, he was able to fulfill the will of God by saving his family during the time of famine.

Joseph had Jehovah's favor from the start. God calls whom He will—it is not us who are worthy but Him in us. But it is still our responsibility to put in the work to show ourselves respectable and trustworthy, to earn a good name with man that can further empower us to do the work God has called us to.

From an early age, I have been blessed with extraordinary favor.

People naturally gravitated toward me and sensed the genuine spirit that I embodied, creating a ripple effect of blessings and opportunities that flowed through my life. When I ultimately surrendered my life to the Lord, everything shifted dramatically. His favor enveloped me like a protective mantle. Experiencing both divine and human favor has been nothing short of transformative. It was as if I had discovered a secret power that ignited my spirit.

You can't fully understand the essence of favor until you bask in the radiance of God's love, which fuels your potential. This divine support empowers me to create paths I never imagined, unveiling a life rich with purpose and opportunity. Favor isn't something we achieve. It is a gift granted by His divine will. It may appear in many forms — unearned blessings, surprise opportunities, or moments of grace amidst trials. Step into the gift and use it to effectively work in the calling wherein you are called.

Take a moment to reflect on a time you experienced the unmistakable favor of God—an outcome or blessing so timely, generous, or unexpected that it bore His signature. Perhaps an unexpected job opportunity that aligned perfectly with your skills and passions, a deep need met at just the right moment, or a door opened when others were closed.

How did you recognize His hand in that moment? What emotions did you feel—gratitude, awe, joy or even unworthiness? Sometimes God's favor surprises us, reminding us that His grace is not something we earn but a gift He gives out of love.

Reflect on how this moment of favor shaped your understanding of God's grace and presence in your life. Did it strengthen your faith, inspire gratitude, or motivate you to extend kindness or support to others in return? Acknowledging and reflecting on such experiences can deepen our relationship with the Lord and remind us of His unwavering goodness.

As you journal, let gratitude lead. Record the experience, offer praise for His goodness, and ask how you might live in a way that reflects the kindness and grace you've received.

Healing

**He heals the brokenhearted and
binds up their wounds.**

◞ PSALM 147:3 [NIV]

ONE NIGHT, I HAD A DREAM in which I found myself sifting through a pile of my jewelry. My task was to untangle necklaces from bracelets, match sets of earrings, and discard anything that appeared old or worn out. As I worked, my frustration grew. The necklaces were so knotted that separating them seemed impossible. In my exasperation, I abandoned my efforts and set the pile of jewelry aside.

Later in the dream, I found myself in a car with a friend who was drunk and unable to give me directions. I was behind the wheel, feeling disoriented in an unfamiliar place. Anxiety rose as I attempted to wake my friend, but she was slumped in the passenger seat, unconscious. As my speed increased uncontrollably, I realized, to my horror, that I was driving in reverse. Eventually, the car slowed and stopped at a manu-facturing warehouse, where a man greeted me outside. Upon entering, I was embraced by an overwhelming sense of peace.

When I inquired of the Holy Spirit about the meaning of my dream, He showed me that it reflected my past. After committing my life to the Lord, I was eager to please Him. Out of excitement, I relied on my strength and knowledge to abandon my old habits. I scrutinized every detail of my life, but this method only caused frustration. The experience of driving in reverse symbolized my reliance on others for direction in life, while God intended for me to move forward through my past swiftly, relying solely on Him. To find peace, I needed to con-front and heal from my past, which was vital for my restoration.

My pastor once said that if trauma remains unaddressed, our souls can freeze at the age the harmful experience occurred. When we are born again, our spirits are revived, bringing us right-side up. Yet we are more than our spirits. God created us with three parts:

1. Body

2. Soul, which includes our feelings and intellect

3. Spirit

While our spirit may experience renewal when we are saved, it does not mean our souls are healed. The trauma I experienced at just three years old left my soul trapped in that moment. Consequently, I was suppressed for many years as further traumas compounded my anguish. The Lord desires to restore everything that the devil has stolen from us, but it will require leaning on Him throughout the entire process.

This journey of healing is an ongoing work, often marked by ups and downs. While we frequently wish to expedite our recovery, the Holy Spirit unveils our traumas in His perfect timing. It's essential to recognize that healing isn't always linear. There have been numerous occasions when I thought I had fully healed, only to have the Holy Spirit unexpectedly bring forgotten wounds to the surface. This revelation can be both daunting and enlightening. The memories and emotions tied to past traumas may resurface when we least expect them, urging us to confront what we thought was behind us. Being open to these revelations is crucial because they serve as guiding lights on our healing journey.

I would be remiss if I said that this process is easy; it certainly isn't. Each revelation can be a painful process that exposes our vulnerabilities. In the medical field, when an old wound isn't healing properly or at considerable risk for infection, it often must undergo a process called debridement. During debridement, a doctor removes dead or damaged tissue from the wound that is harboring bacteria and hindering healing. While the process is often highly painful for the patient, it is necessary for their healing. Jesus is our Great Physician. He understands exactly which old wounds are causing us long term damage and harm. We must be willing to allow Him to go in and clean them out, for our good.

Jeremiah asked, "Is there no balm in Gilead? Is there no physician there? Why then is there no healing for the wound of my people?" (Jer. 8:22) Jesus is not only the Great Physician. He is also our balm of Gilead—a precious, sought-after ointment known for its healing properties and restoration. He is our source for healing, both physical and spiritual.

During these challenging moments of "wound debridement," I learned to rely on the Holy Spirit for strength, comfort, and guidance. Prayer, meditation, and quietude became my companions, providing clarity and assurance, knowing He would soothe all my hurt if I would let Him.

Take a moment to reflect on a time when the Lord revealed an area in your life in desperate need of healing and restoration? What was uncovered? Was it rooted in past hurt, shame, fear, or a broken relationship? How did this revelation come to you?

As you began to walk that healing path, how did God meet you in the process? Did He guide you to a supportive community, lead you into deeper prayer, or perhaps prompt you to pursue counseling or other forms of help? What inner shifts began to take place?

Consider how this journey shaped your soul. What did it teach you about resilience, grace, and the courage it takes to be vulnerable? What did you discover about the character of God as He walked with you?

Healing is rarely instant—it often comes in layers. But each step is a testimony to God's tender, restoring presence. How might reflecting on this experience encourage you to trust Him more deeply today?

_____

_____

_____

_____

_____

_____

_____

Fasting

When you fast, do not look somber as the hypocrites do,
for they disfigure their faces to show others that they are
fasting. Truly, I tell you, they have received their reward
in full. But when you fast, anoint your head and wash your
face, so that it will not be obvious to others that you are
fasting, but only to your Father, who is unseen; and your
Father, who sees what is done in secret, will reward you.

MATTHEW 6:16-18 (NIV)

FASTING IS A SPIRITUAL PRACTICE recorded many times in the scriptures. David and his men fasted as they mourned the loss of Saul and Jonathan. Nehemiah fasted and prayed when he heard about the destruction of Jerusalem. King Jehosophat and the tribe of Judah fasted for deliverance from the Moabites and Ammonites. Fasting was utilized to process grief, give a physical manifestation to internal mourning, to show deep repentance when turning away from sin and back to God, and in combination with prayer for guidance in a decision or deliverance from enemies. Even Jesus fasted in the wilderness for forty days as He spent time in solitude and prayer with His Father.

I often listen to various ministers preach, and a common message is that to experience a supernatural encounter with the Lord, fasting is essential. I've always longed to have my spiritual eyes opened. In my pursuit, I frequently found myself on my knees, crying out to the Lord for a glimpse of the supernatural. However, despite my earnest pleas, He never showed me anything.

When I felt the urge to fast, I began with a three-day fast which, regrettably, ended prematurely. Undaunted, I attempted again. I battled through the hunger but found myself disappointed with the fact I failed to witness anything extraordinary. I observed nothing, and discouragement crept into my spirit.

During my time at church, I heard testimonies about incredible supernatural experiences—people recounting visions of angels, demons, even Jesus, along with other miraculous events—which only fueled my longing. In my frustration, I boldly declared to the Lord my intent to fast for seven days in hopes of a revelation. However, after that week passed, I received no sign. The resulting disillusionment was immense, leaving me feeling disconnected from God. I began to question, "Does God not consider me worthy of a supernatural encounter?"

After many months filled with discouragement, I came across a video featuring a man sharing his personal testimony. He had gone through a similar experience of feeling disheartened in his search for the Lord. This man sought clarity by asking God why he felt let down. In reply, the Lord said, "You fasted for My hands, not for who I am." At that moment, I understood that fasting should not just be about seeking God to reveal Himself in the physical realm. It should focus on nurturing a deeper relationship with Him, concentrating on knowing Him better because He is enough.

Once this man grasped this truth he repented, and over time the Lord unveiled beautiful and wonderful insights to him. After receiving this revelation, I felt a strong urge to repent before the Lord. This act of contrition was not merely about asking for forgiveness; it was also about realigning my heart and intentions with His will. Although I have not yet experienced any sightings of the supernatural, I've come to accept that all things will happen in His perfect timing, dependent on His divine choice. In this current season, my focus is entirely on seeking Him, deepening my relationship with Him, and patiently waiting for His guidance.

This experience taught me that fasting is not a form of spiritual currency with God—as if by giving up this much, He is now obligated to give me that much. Rather, fasting is a way to humble ourselves before the Lord, reminding us of our deep dependence on Him. In fasting, we turn to the God who needs nothing, while our bodies constantly remind us just how much we rely on outward things for survival. It becomes an act of love and worship, elevating God above even our most basic human needs. More than anything, fasting is a tool that softens our hearts and draws us closer to our Creator. By removing something so central to daily life, we create space to rest in Him—finding nourishment for our weary, needy souls.

Fasting invites us into a sacred space of trust and surrender. It a practice of yielding our desires and worries to Him, making space to hear God's voice and embrace His plan as it unfolds. In fasting, we are saying with our bodies, "God, I need You more than anything else."

Take a moment to think back to a time you engaged in the spiritual practice of fasting. Did you enter into the fast with a particular hope, need, or burden in your heart? What prompted you to begin this journey? Maybe you sought clarity, healing, or a breakthrough in a particular aspect of your life. Fasting serves as a powerful means to silence the distractions of daily life, creating room for a deeper connection with God.

During this time, how did the Lord meet you? Were there moments of quiet peace, fresh insight into your prayer life, or a shift in how you viewed a situation?

Often, God's presence reveals itself not in grand gestures but in the small, sacred moments. Pause for a moment to reflect on those experiences. Were there particular moments or insights that made an impression on you during your fast? What did you learn about God's character—or about your own heart? Record what you want to remember about how He revealed Himself to you during that fast.

Revelations from God can be intricately interwoven into our everyday lives, invited in particularly when we make space through sacrifice.

_____

_____

_____

DAY 25:

Called

**I press on toward the goal to win the prize for which
God has called me heavenward in Christ Jesus.**

PHILIPPIANS 3:14 (NIV)

YOU ARE NOT HERE BY CHANCE. Jesus tells us in John chapter 6 that no one comes to Him unless the Father draws them. You have been chosen by the Father and called out for a specific purpose. No one else can fulfill the calling for which God has called you to do.

Though I believed with all my heart God had chosen me to walk this path, I continued to find myself drawn to worldly temptations. The struggle between good and evil felt like an ongoing tug-of-war within my soul. Sometimes, we need to remind ourselves of our calling.

One night, I awoke as if I were in a trance and found myself sitting on the grass in a park. In the park's center were train tracks, with people perched on both sides with Benny Hinn among them, preaching passionately to the assembly.

As I reclined on the grass, two figures flanked me. The figure on my right emanated purity, joy, and love, and brought a deep sense of comfort and peace. Conversely, the figure on my left radiated lust and greed, creating a confusing presence that simultaneously attracted and repelled me. This figure frequently reached out to me, and its touch sparked a troubling blend of emotions. Despite my revulsion, I found myself drawn to it, even kissing its hand at one moment, which added to my internal tumult.

Recognizing the chaos stirring within me, I eventually distanced myself from the presence on my left, finding comfort with the being on my right. I turned to this more virtuous entity and began kissing its hand, letting waves of joy and love envelop me. Meanwhile, the being on my left continued to rub my back—an unpleasant and unwelcome feeling, sharply contrasting the affection I craved from its counterpart. As I struggled with these opposing forces, I felt trapped in a familiar spiritual war, fighting between desire and aversion, purity, and corruption.

Eventually, Benny Hinn announced that everyone should gather water for an upcoming journey. Excited by the idea of adventure, I got up from the grass and looked for a container to collect water but found nothing suitable. Benny Hinn saw me struggling and, with a playful smile said, "Here, take my bottle; there's still some water in it. It's anointed, so be sure to give a seed before drinking." He added, "The Lord will guide you on what seed to offer." The preacher's humorous and warm words filled me with deep gratitude. As I accepted the bottle, I felt the weight of his generosity and began to ponder the importance of giving a seed. Concern washed over me as I realized that, in the dream, I had no money to offer.

In the next moment, I was on stage alongside Benny Hinn at one of his crusades. I placed a beautiful red rug, accented with splashes of yellow and blue, beside him. Taking a moment to kneel on the vibrant rug, I braced myself for the possibility of being asked to step down. To my astonishment, he welcomed my presence as if it were completely normal, as though I had always belonged there.

In that surreal moment on stage, I was surrounded by a vibrant atmosphere and distinctly heard the Lord's voice. He guided me on the exact amount I was meant to give. A wave of clarity washed over me, banishing my previous anxieties about having nothing to offer. With newfound determination, I emerged from that trance-like state, infused with a deep sense of obedience. Without a moment's hesitation, I prepared to donate the specific amount revealed to me. This act of obedience felt like a response to divine guidance and seemed part of a greater purpose unveiled in that moment of spiritual insight.

In pursuing this calling, I experienced a profound sense of peace and fulfillment, recognizing that my actions were in harmony with what had been entrusted to me. This journey enhanced my grasp of faith and reinforced the significance of heeding divine guidance, allowing me to face the path ahead with an open and generous heart.

In addition to providing monetary clarity, the other aspects of the dream were incredibly significant for me as well. I came to understand that while I felt immense joy and peace when I centered my attention on the Lord, resisting the world's allure was still challenging. Benny Hinn, known for his healing, symbolized a divine chance for renewal in my life. His ministry emerged as a powerful emblem in my dream. Drinking from his blessed water felt like a clear message from the Lord indicating a spiritual cleansing—an invitation to be washed and to release the burdens I carried.

Being on stage symbolized my calling to a greater purpose. Kneeling on the vibrant rug added further depth as the red signified deliverance and grace, blue represented wisdom, and yellow embodied understanding and healing. Together, these colors depicted the gifts bestowed upon me by the Lord.

Furthermore, giving a seed represented a spiritual exchange, a gesture that profoundly resonated within the spirit realm. This idea highlights sacrifice, illustrating that genuine growth and healing often demand that we let go of something precious. This dream reflected my internal battles, my desire for a divine connection, and the crucial actions I needed to undertake on my spiritual path. Throughout this experience, I felt a comforting assurance that the Lord was guiding me—encouraging me to accept my calling with appreciation and faith.

The Lord revealed my situation and path. God provides insights into our destination, offering hope for the future. Yet, our journey is about experiences with Him and steadfast faith. Though the way may seem unclear, we can find comfort in knowing our next steps are with him. Paul said in Romans 8:30 "And those he predestined, he also called; those he called, he also justified; those he justified, he also glorified." The apostle also assures us in his letter to the church in Philippi that He who began a good work in us will complete it.

You are called by the Father. He will justify you, reveal your path, and help you walk it to completion in glory if you will let go of that which hinders and embrace Him wholeheartedly.

Reflect on a time when you yearned for clarity in a significant life decision—such as a career change or challenging relationship. Amid uncertainty, how did you learn to release control? Surrendering to God's will requires an open heart and often demands we let go of our expectations for how things "should" unfold.

How did you step outside your comfort zone and allow yourself to trust Him, even when the outcome was unclear? Were your feelings mixed with fear, hope, or even peace?

Consider the practical ways you embraced that vulnerability. Did you lean into prayer, seek guidance through Scripture, or ask for wisdom from others in your faith community? As you surrendered, were there moments when God revealed His direction through circumstances, divine timing or a peace that passes understanding?

Letting go is rarely easy, but it transforms our relationship with God, deepening trust in His wisdom and goodness. Take a moment now to journal about a time when you surrendered to God's will. How did He meet you there, and how did that experience shape your faith?

Perseverance

Consider it pure joy, my brothers and sisters, whenever
you face trials of many kinds, because you know that
the testing of your faith produces perseverance.
Let perseverance finish its work so that you may
be mature and complete, not lacking anything.

JAMES 1:2-4 (NIV)

JAMES' DIRECTIVE TO NOT JUST ENDURE our trials but consider them "pure joy" can be a tough pill to swallow, particularly in life's harshest circumstances. Yet the scriptures make it clear, these are an essential part of our growth as Christians. The tests and trials reveal the state of our hearts and uncovers our deepest beliefs about God while teaching us the truth about His true character. If we walked through with Him, our testing produces the kind of faith that cannot be moved. It is through perseverance His work in us may one day be made complete.

The year I dedicated my life to the Lord turned out to be one of the hardest years of my life. While my circumstances were challenging, I constantly experienced deep comfort, knowing I had the Lord with me. At first, I believed that handing over all my burdens to Jesus would protect me from any negativity. In some ways, I was surrounded by an overflowing sense of peace. But trust me—what I endured was no easy journey!

Before I turned to Jesus, the enemy had no reason to trouble me. I was living my best life (or so I thought) with minimal drama. All that changed once I committed to my faith. The enemy launched countless attacks against me. At my workplace I faced a lawsuit. My finances dwindled alarmingly. Friendships and family relationships endured various struggles. It felt like I could never catch a break. Yet, through all these hardships, I still found peace.

Don't get me wrong; I have plenty of journal entries filled with prayers where I lamented and cried out to the Lord asking, "Why me?!" But even after these pleas, I continued to push forward, only to face the next challenge that arose. Looking back now, I can see that the Lord was showing me glimpses of what I would endure long before I encountered those trials. He was preparing me for what was to come. While I was in the midst of turmoil, I didn't recognize His hand at work. Now I understand that He was steadfastly guiding me and keeping me through the storm.

James also said "Blessed"—which means favored by God and spiritually fulfilled— "is the one who perseveres under trial because, having stood the test, that person will receive the crown of life that the Lord has promised to those who love Him." (James 1:12) We run not for what we will receive in this life, but for our eternal reward. Even so, our God is indeed a good God. He is actively moving here on earth today, even when we cannot see His work ourselves. The Lord does not promise us a life free from hardship; in fact, He warns us that our time on earth will be filled with trials and tribulations. Yet amid the struggles and challenges, He assures us true joy and peace can flourish when we keep Him at the center of our lives. This beautiful paradox reveals the strength that comes from leaning on Him during our most difficult moments.

Think back to a season when you faced a significant struggle. What hardships or a challenges did you encounter during this time—personal loss, health problems, family issues, or intense stress?

In those moments of uncertainty and pain, how did you experience God's presence? Was there a Scripture that brought comfort and encouragement during your darkest times? Did prayer give you peace, allowing you to feel His peace wrap around you like a warm blanket?

Perhaps His support came through the people around you—friends, family, or a community that reminded you that you were not alone. Even during hardship, were there any moments of unexpected joy or clarity? How did these moments shift your perspective?

As you reflect on these seasons of struggle, consider how your relationship with the Lord deepened. Often, in the furnace of trials that our faith is refined, and we emerge stronger with a deeper appreciation of His goodness.

_____

_____

_____

_____

_____

_____

DAY 27:

Prophecies

**Do not treat prophecies with contempt but
test them all; hold on to what is good.**

1 THESSALONIANS 5:20-21 (NIV)

WHEN JESUS LEFT THIS EARTH, He didn't leave His followers wondering
or wandering. He left them with specific instructions to wait until
they were endued with power—filled with the Spirit on the day of
Pentecost. It was then that the Church was established. Paul told the
believers in Ephesus that when Jesus ascended, He gave the Church
apostles, prophets, evangelists, pastors, and teachers. The work of these
individuals is not to promote themselves, but to build up the body of
Christ "until we all reach unity in the faith and in the knowledge of the
Son of God and become mature, attaining to the whole measure of the
fullness of Christ" (Eph. 4:13).

While some hear the word "prophet" and immediately think of

the men and women of the Old Testament, Paul makes it clear that the prophetic ministry is very much alive within the Church—even after Jesus' ascension. If it was active then, it remains active now. As Hebrews 13:8 reminds us, "Jesus Christ is the same yesterday and today and forever." His gifts to the Church have not changed.

The church I go to can be described as a prophetic church, where the congregation often receives prophetic messages during each service. I clearly recall the first prophetic word I received after I committed my life to the Lord. It was revealed to me that I would become a prophetess, gifted with the spirit of discernment and empowering me to heal and cast out demons.

At that moment, I experienced a blend of awe and disbelief. Before this prophecy was declared over my life, I had been receiving dreams that I found difficult to interpret. However, once the prophetic message was shared, everything started to fall into place. Still, I struggled to picture myself embracing such a calling. I thought, "Me? I can't recall a single verse! I can barely pray for a few minutes, and I just don't know enough."

Even when the Lord reveals our destinies, He does so without illuminating the entire path. He shows us only enough to guide us one step at a time. Although I questioned my abilities, I decided to allow the Lord to work in my life. To my surprise, He presented opportunities seldom available to those new to the faith. I was invited to participate in the church's leadership training group and transitioned from being an usher to a stage manager. I found myself among women who were further along in their faith to offer guidance and support for my spiritual development.

While I recognized God was hastening my journey, I often felt inferior and unworthy of the mantle He was placing upon me. This feeling of inadequacy made me withdraw. I let fear and doubt infiltrate my thoughts, suggesting that I wasn't ready. Yet, the Lord anticipated this.

It took my stepping back to understand that I needed more patience and a deeper grasp of my identity in Christ before I could fully accept the calling before me. Since then, I have received numerous prophetic words that have come to pass. I firmly believe that one day, God will fulfill the work He has begun in me.

The opening scripture for today's entry heeds us to test prophecies. John echoed this sentiment in I John 4:1 with a warning to "not believe every spirit but test the spirits to see whether they are from God, because many false prophets have gone out into the world." Jesus warned us of false prophets that come in sheep's clothing, appearing docile and innocent, but are ravenous wolves quick to devour. Indeed, as Christians we must be harmless as doves but wise as serpents. Pray as Solomon did, asking for wisdom to discern between a true prophetic word and that of a false prophet. And test the prophecies. If a prophetic word goes directly against God's written Word, it is not of Him. He is immutable. His Word cannot lie.

A prophetic word serves to confirm what the Lord has already conveyed to you. It acts as a beacon, strengthening the journey you're on and motivating you to stay firm in your faith. Seek God's wisdom and guidance for proper interpretation and fulfilment in your life as you keep Him at the center.

Think back to a time when someone spoke a prophetic word over your life. How did that word resonate with you in the moment? Was it a message that ignited hope and excitement, or did it raise questions and stir anticipation?

As you recall that experience, reflect on how the prophetic word aligned with your understanding of God's will for your life. Did it reflect something you had already sensed or believed the Lord had revealed to you? Has this word come to fruition yet? If so, what signs or confirmations have you observed along the way?

If it hasn't yet come to pass, think about your journey since that moment. What guidance or direction have you received from the Lord as you move closer to the fulfillment of His? Perhaps you've experienced personal growth, new opportunities, or key lessons that have shaped your character and faith. Have mentors or supportive friends come alongside you to help you in this process?

In what ways has your trust in Him deepened as you await the realization of His word?

Remember that timing is just as integral to God's plan as the promises themselves. While waiting can be a challenge, it is also a time for preparation and intimacy with the Lord. Take a moment to reflect on the lessons you've learned during this waiting period. How have you seen God shape and mold you as you await the fulfillment of His word?

Seasons

**There is a time for everything and a season
for every activity under the heavens.**

ECCLESIASTES 3:1 (NIV)

THE IDEA OF A JOURNEY to follow the Lord is meaningful in various respects. Some individuals might view their relationship with Christ as a linear path. While it's crucial to keep progressing, we must also appreciate that each of us goes through different seasons along this journey. Every season we go through is meant for His glory and is intended to deepen our relationship with Him. Some seasons might last longer than others, and certain ones may present specific challenges. Recognizing the current season allows us to move forward with unfolding insights.

In my last season, I centered on themes of redemption, forgiveness, and healing. Everything the Lord revealed to me revolved around these concepts. After spending 17 years without acknowledging Him, it was essential for the Lord to restore the lost time in my life. To move into the next dimension of His glory, I had to learn important lessons in forgiveness and healing.

As I enter this new season, God is teaching me about patience. He is guiding me to depend less on my understanding. Even as I write this book, I feel uncertain about its ultimate purpose. What does He want me to do with it? In the past, I would have fixated on the next ten steps. But now, understanding the season I'm in, I realize God wants me to be obedient and let things unfold in their own timing.

Additionally, He reveals that I don't need to do anything extraordinary to hear and see Him; I simply need to ask. While fasting, sacrificing, and planting seeds (sowing and serving in ministry) are all meaningful practices, the Lord is emphasizing that He is good to me regardless of my actions during this season. He is fostering a profound desire within me to know His Word, which leads me to a deeper understanding of Him. The more I comprehend Him, the more gratitude fills my heart. My challenges seem minor in the light of His greatness. In this season, my priorities are obedience, patience, and understanding.

Understanding our past and current seasons illuminates the ultimate purpose of our lives. This awareness empowers us to navigate life's challenges with confidence, knowing that our circumstances are temporary and ever-changing. Each season, whether joyful or difficult, serves a distinct purpose in shaping who we are and preparing us for what lies ahead.

As you come upon a time of change in your life, whether it coincides with the turning of the calendar to a new year or not, it can be helpful to reflect on the past season and assign a few words of remembrance to it. What did God seem to be most focused on shifting during that time? He's always working in us and for us. Some words to consider include but are not limited to renewal, transformation, rooted, sanctification, surrender, humility, courage, obedience, purpose, breakthrough, fruit-fulness, rest, presence.

Next, Take time to pray over your current or upcoming season, and ask the Lord to guide you in choosing new words or specific areas He wants you to focus your time and energy on. If He leads you to a season of rest, let that shape your decisions. Learn to say no to extra commitments, trusting that rest is His priority for you right now—even if that changes in the next season. God's timing often doesn't mean "no," but "not yet." If your word is *sanctification*, it may be time to clear out the noise and distractions that are pulling you away from deeper intimacy with Him. Even if something isn't sinful, He might be asking you to release it because it's hindering your growth. This could be your moment to let go—your invitation to surrender. Open your heart, stretch out your hands, and let Him lead.

Look back over some of the more significant seasons of your life. What lessons did they impart? You may recall struggles that challenged you to confront deep-rooted fears or insecurities. Such experiences often act as catalysts for growth, helping us to discover strengths we didn't know we had. Were there also seasons of joy and fulfillment that highlighted the value of relationships, expressing gratitude, or living in line with your core values? Each season builds upon the previous one, weaving a unique tapestry of experiences that enrich our spiritual journey.

Now, consider how those past lessons are shaping the season you're in today. Have certain themes or challenges emerged? Perhaps you are cultivating patience in the face of uncertainty, trusting that God has a divine plan, even when life feels chaotic. Maybe you're deepening your understanding of love and forgiveness or learning to offer grace to yourself and others. Is this season teaching you to establish healthier boundaries or see vulnerability as a strength?

Take a moment to reflect on specific instances where you've seen God focusing on a particular aspect of your life during this season. How has He been shaping you through these experiences?

Next, ask God to reveal a word or theme for your current season. What is He highlighting for you right now? Write it down and place it somewhere visible to remind yourself of His presence and guidance as you move through this season.

Gifts

To one there is given through the Spirit a message
of wisdom, to another a message of knowledge by
means of the same Spirit, to another faith by the
same Spirit, to another gift of healing by that one
Spirit, to another miraculous power, to another
prophecy, to another distinguishing between spirits,
to another speaking in different kinds of tongues,
and to still another the interpretation of tongues.

1 CORINTHIANS 12:8-10 (NIV)

WHEN JESUS PHYSICALLY LEFT THIS EARTH, He didn't leave us without hope and help. He promised the Church the Holy Spirit, a five-fold ministry and gifts that would be given to all. These gifts are not only for our own benefit, but for the edification of the body of Christ. Each one has its perfect work and purpose in our lives and in the community of believers.

While some may have different understanding about what it means to receive the Holy Spirit, I believe in an experience reflective of what is recorded in Acts 2, including speaking in tongues. I recall being nine years old when my father took the time to explain the significance of speaking in my heavenly language. I frequently listened to him pray during the early hours of the night, his foreign tongue spoken with such fervor that the whole house seemed to tremble. Raised in a Pentecostal church, I understood the concept of speaking in tongues on a surface level, but I lacked the knowledge on how to truly receive this gift.

After my father read about the Day of Pentecost in Acts 2, he asked if I wanted to receive the gift of speaking in tongues. I agreed though I didn't fully understand how it would happen. My father placed his hand on my belly and prayed in his heavenly language for what felt like two or three hours though it was likely much shorter. Eventually, two syllables slipped out. My father celebrated and encouraged me to continue, which I did. As I grew older, those two syllables evolved into a words.

One might assume that after 17 years the language would have faded. Yet, when I recommitted my life to the Lord, His irrevocable gift of those very words returned to me. I found that the more I expressed those words and let the Holy Spirit guide me, the more they morphed into sentences. Depending on my level of immersion in prayer, it could even evolve into an entirely different language. Regardless of these variations, speaking in my heavenly language offers me a more profound prayer experience than I ever thought possible.

Often, my heart is heavy with the weight of this life and the needs of my own family or those around me. I come to God and, at times, fail to find the words to pray about the burden I feel. Paul told the Church in Romans 8 that this is exactly where the Holy Spirit steps in—interceding for us when we don't even know the words to pray. In a previous chapter we talked about praying within God's will. This is accomplished by praying in the Spirit. "And He who searches our

190

hearts knows the mind of the Spirit, because the Spirit intercedes for God's people in accordance with the will of God" (Rom. 8:27).

Even our worship is to be Spirit-led: "... the true worshipers will worship the Father in the Spirit and in truth..." (John 4:23)

The Holy Spirit may grant us gifts even before we wholeheartedly commit to the Lord. Some may have a deep understanding of what someone else is experiencing, commonly known as the "gift of knowledge" that God will use to tend to the hurting hearts of His people. Other gifts may come to those who earnestly seek and request the Lord to reveal them in our lives. Remember, they are gifts. We cannot earn them. It is God who gives, because of His love and grace, and He alone determines what He will pour out on whom and when. Regardless of how we recognize them, all His gifts are given without repentance, reaffirming that they are intended for our faith journey.

Have you ever sensed that God has given you a unique way to serve others? Spiritual gifts often show up in moments of clarity, encouragement, or a quiet inner prompting to act.

Think back—how did you begin to recognize your spiritual gifts? Was there a strong inner pull to comfort others, lead or teach? Did someone in your community affirm a strength they saw in you? Often, our gifts are discovered in relationship with others helping us to see what God has already placed within us.

Once you began to recognize those gifts, what steps did you take to grow in them? Did you spend time in prayer and fasting, seeking God's guidance? Maybe you sought mentorship in your church or engaged in workshops to nurture and refine these abilities.

This journey requires stepping out of your comfort zone—volunteer for something new, embrace challenging roles, or take on responsibilities that stretch your faith.

Now, reflect on how you're currently use your gifts for God's glory. Are you involved in a ministry where your strengths are being used in teaching, counseling, worship, or hospitality? Perhaps your knowledge aids others during Bible studies or personal discipleship.

Every act, big or small, is significant in God's kingdom and reflects your desire to serve Him and others. As you journal today, ask God to show you how He wants to use your gifts in this season. Write down what you feel Him speak into and let that awareness guide your prayers and your willingness to step forward in faith.

The Race

**I have fought the good fight, I have finished the race,
I have kept the faith.**

2 TIMOTHY 4:7 (NIV)

THIS JOURNEY YOU ARE ON may be just beginning, or it may be a race you have been running for many years. I've come to realize an important truth: God can only do what we are willing to allow Him to do in our lives. Availability and willingness are the greatest assets we can bring. He can do anything in us and through us if we make the space for Him to work. This is not a 200-meter dash. We are participating in the marathon of our lives, and the ultimate goal is to finish that race in close communion with Him.

This final day's entry is dedicated to reinforcing your declaration of faith and lifelong commitment to the Lord. Read these words aloud as an affirmation or write your own to state your resolve to follow Him, no matter what. Words have power. Speaking a resolution like this aloud daily or weekly does something to the connections in the human brain, reinforcing the words in a way that merely reading silently cannot.

From now on, I affirm that I will fully embrace every aspect of this journey with faith and purpose. I commit to completely surrendering my will and desires to Him, recognizing that genuine fulfillment arises from aligning my life with His purpose.

I declare over my life a posture of openness and receptivity. I will nurture a heart eager to hear His voice and follow His guidance. Daily, I will seek His presence with intentionality, understanding that it is in that intimate space where my strength and direction arise. I desire to be a vessel for His light and love, radiating brightly in a world that is in dire need of hope.

Furthermore, I commit to welcoming challenges and setbacks as opportunities for growth. Rather than perceiving obstacles as hindrances, I will regard them as stepping stones that enhance my character and bolster my faith. I will embrace discomfort, trusting that in the fire God is refining and shaping me into the person He intended me to be.

This race will be run through grace, strengthened by my dedication to endurance and perseverance, aware that the journey isn't always simple. I will rely on God's promises, reminding myself that He WILL complete the good work He has begun in me (Phil. 1:6). His Word cannot lie. As I run this race, I will engage with a community of believers, gathering strength and encouragement from those on a similar journey. Accountability and support will serve as my allies as I pursue the finish line.

I dedicate myself to the ongoing renewal of my mind through God's Word, allowing scripture to guide my thoughts and shape my actions. Meditating on His truths will be my source of strength and inspiration, especially in times of difficulty. I will prioritize prayer, recognizing it as my lifeline to God—a place where I find clarity, resilience, and the grace to face each day's challenges.

Ultimately, I choose to let my life reflect His grace and love. As I complete this race, I hope to hear the words I deeply desire. "Well done, good and faithful servant."

My journey is more than just attaining the end goal. It is about nurturing my relationship with Him throughout. With each step I aim to glorify God, believing that He will guide me to my ultimate fulfillment in Him. In this commitment, I discover hope for the journey ahead, for the races still to come, and for the amazing plans God has laid out for my life.

In Jesus name, Amen!

Paul described the Christian life as a race marked by endurance, perseverance, and wholehearted trust in God. As you reflect today, consider the many ways you've experienced this spiritual journey. Whether in seasons of struggle or strength, each step has shaped your walk with the Lord.

Can you recall a time when you felt you were truly "fighting the good fight" in your faith? What did that season teach you about endurance and reliance in God?

Reflect on a moment when surrendering to God's will was difficult. How did that experience shape your trust in His timing and plan? What was a challenge or setback you faced in your spiritual journey? How did God help you overcome it, and what growth came from it? Think of a time where you felt God speaking to you or guiding you. How did you respond, and what did that teach you about listening and obedience?

Record a time when God's promises sustained you. Was there a specific scripture or truth that helped you push forward?

Who has been a source of spiritual encouragement for you? How has community helped you stay the course in your Christian walk? What habits or practices help you stay grounded in God's Word? How might you deepen those rhythms so that Scripture becomes greater influence in your daily life?

As you journal today, ask God to renew your strength for the race ahead. What's one step of faith He's calling you to take right now?

Conclusion

I can do all this through Him who gives me strength.

PHILIPPIANS 4:13

WHEN THE LORD CALLS ME TO A TASK, it usually feels daunting and over-whelming. Whether it's a simple request or a significant assignment, there's a sense of weight that accompanies it. Throughout the journey of obedience, I frequently grapple with doubts. Am I capable of this? Do I have what it takes for this challenge? It's a struggle that many of us understand—a tug-of-war between our insecurities and the divine calling in our hearts.

I've been entrusted with a significant responsibility to write my own book about my journey with Christ that captures my spiritual experience in a profound way.

It felt intimidating. Yet, I recognize the value and impact of a book. It has an enduring quality, capable of spanning generations by providing insights, encouragement, and wisdom to future readers. It transforms into a lasting legacy and shares a piece of my spirit that I hope can inspire others for many years ahead.

As I pondered this call, I recognized that I must not let this moment slip away. Each instance spent reflecting on my journey offered a chance to reveal the divine connections that have influenced my life, showcasing God's faithfulness, guidance, and transformative strength. My narrative, which comprises my triumphs, challenges, and lessons, holds the power to inspire others who might be traversing similar paths or encountering related obstacles. Writing also uncovers profound truth. Through articulating my experiences, I often unearthed deeper insights into my own faith. This practice became a therapeutic reflection, allowing me to recount moments of grace, doubt, clarity, and confusion that have shaped my identity. Documenting each chapter of my spiritual journey inevitably led me to heal and understand.

I pray this book has done that for you as well. Through the questions and writing space provided, I hope that it has been an opportunity for you to reflect on who you are in Christ and remember all the ways He has been faithful.

Now go and press on, embracing the challenge ahead with confidence in your Savior. Lay your doubts before the Lord, asking for His strength to conquer your insecurities. Remember, you are not alone. He empowers those He calls and grants the wisdom and courage needed to fulfill your purpose. Writing this book is not just an obligation; it is an act of obedience, a contribution to God's narrative in your life, and a gift for those who may benefit from it. Along your journey, commit to revealing your true self, recognizing that vulnerability fosters connection and encouragement.

At its core, committing to expressing his truth and sharing your experiences for the glory of God and the benefit of those who follow. Let your narrative serve as a beacon, shedding light on the way for others and encouraging them to contemplate their own journeys with Christ. Throughout this process, maintain your faith that this endeavor will yield results beyond your expectations. The Lord is by your side and will provide you with strength.

If this journal has blessed you in any way, we kindly ask you to leave a review on the platform where you received it and share it with someone who may need it. Your words have power—and every review helps more people discover the impact of this message.

All proceeds from this journal go directly to the Sponsorship Fund at The 1 and Only, which supports individuals who have a story to tell but lack the financial means to publish their book. By leaving a review and spreading the word, you're not only encouraging others—you're helping to make it possible for more testimonies to be written, published, and shared for God's glory.

Thank You

May God bless you and keep you
all the days of your life.

www.ingramcontent.com/pod-product-compliance
Lightning Source LLC
Chambersburg PA
CBHW061742120626
46550CB00005B/1860